First printing, 1982
Second printing, 1991
Third printing, 1994
All Rights Reserved

Copyright 1982
by Kripalu Yoga Fellowship

Library of Congress Catalog Card Number: 82-83357
ISBN: 0-940258-07-2

Printed in the United States of America
by Kripalu Publications
P.O. Box 793
Lenox, MA 01240

This was originally published as a commemorative book and,
for this reason, is not being revised in subsequent printings.

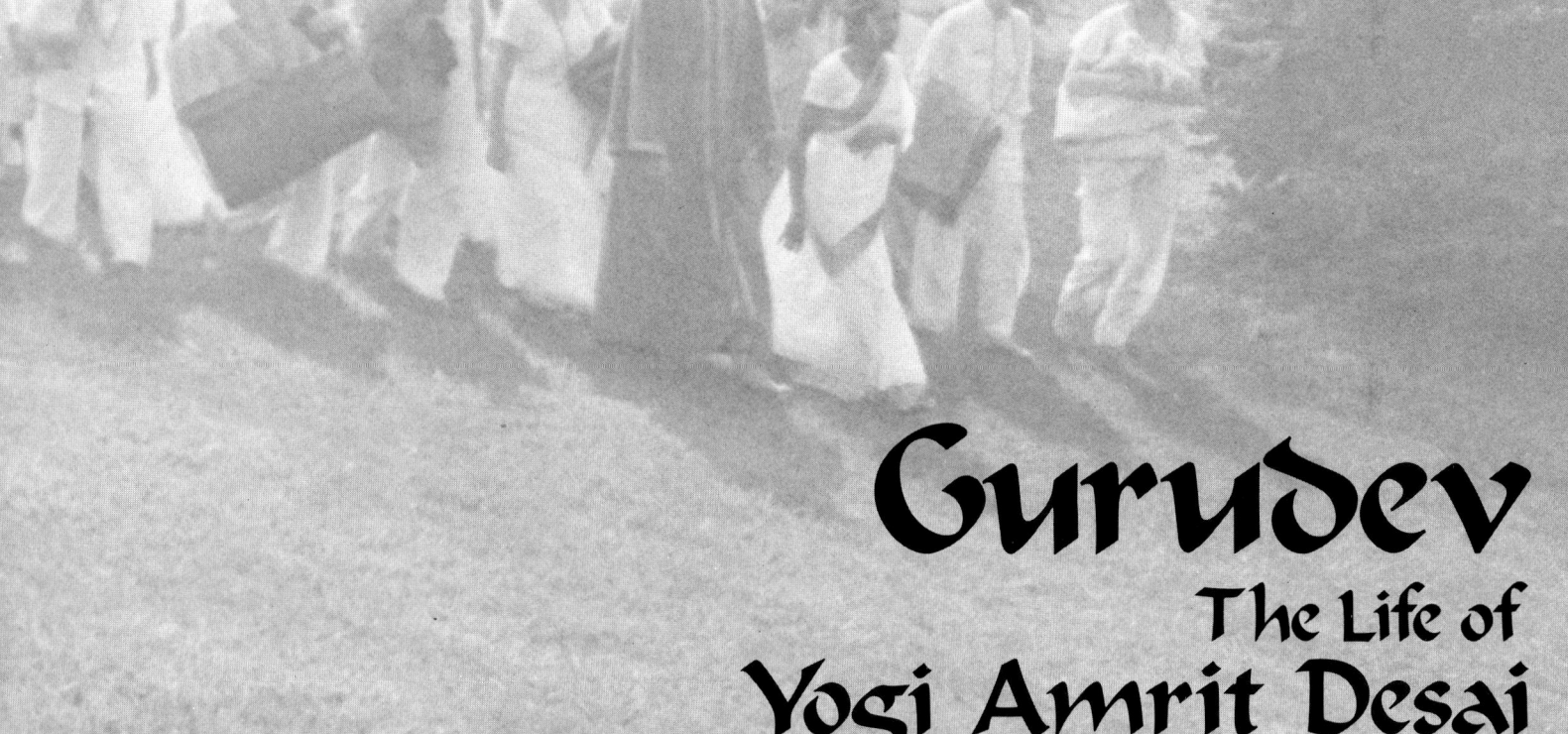

Gurudev
The Life of Yogi Amrit Desai

Gurudev

The Life of
Yogi Amrit Desai

by Sukanya Warren

with Frances Mellen
Peter Mellen

Foreword

Yogi Amrit Desai: my spiritual teacher, my guru. A person whose compassion, brilliance, and life-embracing spirit have illumined the hearts of thousands of Western seekers. Who is this being whose love has so powerfully transformed my life? The question was foremost in my heart as I wrote this book.

In developing this manuscript, I had the special privilege of reliving with Gurudev the richness of his personal story. I came to understand on a deep level his way of encountering life; and I began to know my spiritual teacher more wholly than I had before. In eight years of living in Gurudev's presence, our relationship had taken many forms. At times he had been a mother to me, tender and gentle in his love. At other times, clear and firm in the Truth he represents, he had been a wise father. I had even seen the child in Gurudev, dancing with life, laughing with joy for all that is. But now, through my work on the book, a new understanding of Gurudev lit my mind: I began to comprehend the scope of his service to humanity. With awe I realized the powerful impact his life and teachings have made in the West, and the life-long consistency of his unswerving search for Truth.

Writing this book has affected my own continuing process of self-awareness as well. The project brought me the privilege of working with Gurudev for many hours at a time, exploring the experiences and personal relationships which shaped his life vision. I had the extraordinary opportunity to ask Gurudev all that I had ever wanted to know about him: his fears, his doubts; his moments of greatest happiness; his ways of perceiving his world, himself, and his work in America. At times his very humanness took me by surprise and disarmed me totally. At other times, his inspired vision of life startled me into a new consciousness. Little by little, as I absorbed the pattern of his life, his attitudes began to permeate my own life experiences. His way of responding to life infused my own, affecting my interactions, my decisions, my struggles, and the process of my personal growth. Gurudev's greatest teaching—his life—became my daily scripture.

After the initial research, I was joined on the project by two friends, Ramadevi (Frances Mellen) and Ramakrishna (Peter Mellen). A gifted filmwriter and author, Ramadevi edited and revised the manuscript with inexhaustible dedication. Her inspired work on the book was a source of tremendous support, bringing order and flow to the patchwork quilt of images, stories, and events from Gurudev's life.

An art historian, filmmaker, and author of three major books on art, Ramakrishna made aesthetic and intuitive contributions in the editing and design processes. These contributions and his calm overview, grounded the project in both beauty and direction.

Working together with the fabric of Gurudev's life wove the three of us into a relationship of deep support and love. Miraculously, with the hundreds of hours of work and the usual tight deadlines, there were never conflicts or negative feelings among us on the project. The exploration of Gurudev's life propelled us together into a creative space of gratitude and inner freedom, affecting us in many still-unfolding ways.

In addition to the dedication of Ramadevi and Ramakrishna, I want to acknowledge Devapriya (Patience Howden) who tirelessly spent many hours doing the necessary research in the ashram archives. Her enthusiasm has been as valuable as the practical help she so competently provided. Final acknowledgements and gratitude go to the staff of Kripalu Publications—from photographers and typesetters to printers—who, as always, invested the kind of caring and creative service in the production of the book that Gurudev himself would contribute.

One moment in the creation of the book stands out. Gurudev had spent a long summer afternoon with Ramadevi, Ramakrishna, and myself answering our questions about his relationship to Bapuji, to the young Westerners who flocked to him in the early '70's, and to his personal sadhana and spiritual life. The directness and truth of his answers opened each of us to a deeper level of self-knowing. After Gurudev left, we came back together in the sun-drenched study. For long minutes we sat, hand in hand, gazing at the late afternoon sunlight glinting through the tall pines. Wordlessly, we shared our experiences of the immensity of Gurudev's love, feeling his living presence and our peace as tangibly as we sensed the light washing over us.

Gurudev's life story contains the seeds of a thousand lessons. It has touched and changed my life. It is my hope that, in reading his story, you find Gurudev reaching out to your heart, encircling you with his joy in living, and his profound love.

Sukanya Warren
Summit Station, Pa.
August 15, 1982

Contents

1 · A Boyhood in India 3
2 · Meeting the Master 11
3 · Coming to America 21
4 · Discovering Kripalu Yoga 27
5 · Guru and Disciple 45
6 · Channeling the Energy 63
7 · Bapuji in America 81
8 · The Path of Selfless Service 93
9 · Truth Shines Like the Sun 103

Yogi Amrit Desai: A Chronology 109
Titles and Degrees 112
Art Awards and Exhibits 113
Glossary of Sanskrit Terms 115
Further Reading 117

1·A Boyhood in India

In a western village of Gujarat Province, a young couple, Bhuriben and Chimanlal Desai, welcomed their second son into the world. The day was October 16, 1932. The little boy, with light Indian skin, curling dark hair, and large eyes, was named Amrit, which means "divine nectar of the Gods."

In keeping with Indian tradition, Amrit was born in his grandmother's home, in Halol. Soon afterwards, he and his mother returned to their home in Pratappura, travelling the ten miles between the two villages by bullock cart.

The Desai family life in Pratappura was simple, as it was for the other 250 inhabitants of the rural town. Chimanlal Desai, Amrit's father, was a highly principled man who held a position of respect in the community. He was one of the two shopkeepers in the village and a cultured member of the Vaishya (merchant) class.

The family's store was a 12' × 15' screened veranda attached to the front of the small house. Only the most basic of staple goods were available, and trade was carried on by barter. A townswoman would bring in a small portion of peanuts or grain from the fields. Carefully unwrapping these precious goods, she would place them on the scale to be weighed, and exchange them for a few ounces of oil, salt or rice. A more fortunate farmer, able to store grain from his ten acres of land, might bring in enough millet to trade for luxuries such as tea, sugar, potatoes or onions. Among the villagers—farmers, fishermen, potters and laborers—almost no one could afford green vegetables of any kind. Chimanlal often extended credit to poor families; he ran his modest business with high standards and a kind heart.

It is in Pratappura that Amrit's fondest childhood memories are rooted. The family—Bhuriben and Chimanlal, their oldest son Ramanlal (who died at age sixteen of typhoid), Amrit, Shanti, and daughters Hiraben, Pemilaben, Manuben, and Ushaben—all lived together in their one room home, one of the finest in the village. Amrit recalls his childhood home:

The house in which we lived had earthen walls and floor, and a tin roof. Our home was one large room, with a partition made of cans which held our cooking grains. On one side of the room was a storage area filled with burlap bags of goods for my father's store. Next to this area was a space for the handmade cots on which we all slept. In the middle of the house was a large swing, a common thing in Indian homes. For cooking, there was a fireplace dug into the earth. There were no

At left: Family portrait with Amrit's father Chimanlal, Amrit, his youngest sister Ushaben, and his mother Bhuriben.

rugs, no pictures, only one armchair, and no wall hangings. We lived an extremely primitive life. I loved it... and I was very loved by my family.

The family's daily activities consisted of a plain, life-sustaining routine. Every morning at 4 a.m., Chimanlal would rise and light the fire to heat the family's bath water, drawn from the village well and stored in large earthen pots. After the fire was started, Chimanlal would light his hookah (water pipe) and settle back to smoke his tobacco until the bath was ready. After having bathed and dressed, he would perform puja (worship) to Shri Radha-Krishna, the deity of the Vaishnav religion, while chanting "Shri Krishna Charanam Mama" ("I surrender to Lord Krishna").

Amrit remembers awakening to the beautiful sounds which broke the silence of his early morning sleep.

Every morning I would awaken on my cot to the sound of the hookah bubbling and gurgling. I could hear the crackle of the fire, and the sweet smell of the fire's smoke would fill the room. My mother would grind her flour early in the morning. There were two round stones, with a hole in the center into which she would constantly feed the grain. She would turn the upper stone by a handle to grind the grain into flour. The whole time she was preparing the grain, she would sing bhajans. I would awaken to her sweet voice, the sound of the turning stones, and the songs of the birds. We also had water buffalos for milk when I was little; so some mornings, my mother and father would be churning the milk into yogurt with a device constructed of ropes on a pulley connected to a pot with churning blades. I loved the yogurt and butter, and especially the sweetballs.

Amrit and the other children rose at five in the morning, washed, and cleaned their teeth with twigs. After chanting prayers, they had their breakfast and went out to play. Sometimes Amrit would follow his mother to the creek where she did her laundry, for he loved to be outside observing nature. From the clay on the banks of the creek, he would make little animals— peacocks, elephants, and parrots—letting them dry in the sun for later use as toys. At 10 a.m. the family had their lunch together. When the sunbeams came through a hole in the tin roof, and fell on a certain spot on the wall, Amrit would say, "Mama, it's time to go to school." With the other village children, Amrit walked 1½ miles to the school in Shankarpura, picking and eating berries along the way. Classes were held in a one-room schoolhouse, in which one teacher was responsible for all five grades.

In the evening, Chimanlal would close his shop, and gather his family around the family swing. Carefully he would open the prized copy of the *Mahabharata*, and read to his children stories of the noble Arjuna, the Pandava brothers, and the teachings of Lord Krishna.

In the winter evenings, we'd gather in a circle around an earthen brazier, in which my brothers and I had built a small fire. In our small house, with the winter cold outside, we would cuddle together, and my father would read to us from the Mahabharata. *At other times, he read from the* Ramayana *and other scriptures. Every day, no matter what I was doing, I was always dreaming of where the story would go next. We were all eager to hear the continuation of this fantastic epic. Our young imaginations were tremendous, and the entire scene of every story would come alive in my mind more vividly than a movie. My father had such a beautiful voice, and these scriptures were written in a poetic way. His readings were music to my heart and ears.*

Top left: (clockwise from upper left) Chimanlal, Amrit's oldest sister Hiraben, Bhuriben, Amrit (age 1), and his older brother Ramanlal.
Bottom left: A street in Pratappura.
Above: Chimanlal and Bhuriben Desai.

Above: Amrit at age 14.
Top right: (clockwise from left) Two relatives, Bhuriben, Chimanlal, and Amrit.
Bottom right: Kitchen in Amrit's house in Halol.

When Amrit was ten, the family moved to Halol, in part for him to continue his education at secondary school. Only recently recovered from a debilitating three-month bout with typhoid which nearly took his life, Amrit spent long hours under Chimanlal's guidance learning how to walk again. Once he had recovered, he had a bewildering introduction to the more sophisticated world of the larger town (population 17,000). He entered his new school and neighborhood where the way of communicating, the norms of school and social life, dress and classroom behavior, were all unfamiliar to him.

I had a disconnected feeling when we moved to Halol. I didn't understand what was going on around me. I had been a good student at Pratappura, and suddenly my grades fell. But once I caught up with my new environment, I became very sharp. What I lacked in social skills, I had gained tenfold in living a very experiential existence. From my upbringing, my mind was uncluttered and perceptive, and when I became comfortable in my new surroundings, my grades became excellent — not first in my class, because I preferred playing to studying — but always at the top level.

I was chosen to be class monitor, to maintain discipline in the classroom when the teacher was out. This must have been the philosophy of reforming the mischievous with the most mischievous. I would stand before the class, and when someone talked or acted out-of-line, I would say, pointing at him, 'You, go there,' and send him into the corner of the room to wait until the teacher returned. Yet, I myself was the prime mischief-maker in the class. When the teacher turned to the blackboard, I would cleverly distort the meaning of his words. My friends would all laugh, and the teacher would not know who the instigator was or why everyone was laughing."

Throughout his boyhood, Amrit had a profound attraction for all types of self-improvement and personal growth. Inspired by his father, who had been an outstanding wrestler and who had a fine physique, Amrit started to read books on physical fitness and body building. Every day he practiced exercises outside his home. An old man, who daily noted his persistence as he watched from a neighboring house, said, "Some day Amrit will be a very famous and successful man." But there were many frustrations for the young boy:

I wanted to work on myself and to grow so much. I felt very inhibited in this desire and suffocated in my search for self-expansion. I wanted to read, but books were scarce. I longed to travel and to see more than our village, but there was no money. I wanted to build up my body, but there were no teachers. Our family couldn't afford enough highly nutritious food, or even a daily glass of milk. I also wanted to grow spiritually, but where could I go? What I could not know, was that all of this was preparing me for Bapuji.

Such unsatisfied longings served to intensify Amrit's desire to grow and deepened his ability to utilize every resource within his grasp for furthering his development. When a self-improvement book was available, Amrit read it and re-read it, writing down the most significant parts and practicing, practicing, practicing. At age 15, reading a Gujarati translation of Dale Carnegie's *How to Win Friends and Influence People*, he was deeply impressed. He saw within the book's philosophy a way to live which accentuated the positive in every situation, and which remained sensitive to others' needs. Amrit memorized and practiced the techniques as a scripture for positive living, rather than for financial success. Inspiring his sisters with the notes from his readings, he would teach them and say, "You must practice this. It is very important. It will change your life."

With his determination and natural abilities, Amrit also developed his athletic abilities. He had a passion for play and sports that drew him into the fields of Halol during every free moment. Noting his resistance to studying and his preference for sports and play, his mother Bhuriben would occasionally scold him with the timeless maxim, "You must study well, Amrit. If you don't study, no one will even hire you to wash dishes in a restaurant."

In his early teens, Amrit met his friends after school daily for sports and games, often playing alone against all the other boys—up to twenty of them. His remarkable speed and skill invariably made him the winner. Finally, the other boys outlawed him from the team because he was so invincible.

On weekends, Amrit led his group of neighborhood friends on hikes up the highest mountain near the village. It was on this same mountain that, in earlier years, his father had worked as a munitions supervisor for a British mining company. More importantly, this was the legendary Pavagadh Mountain, the place where the great sage Vishwamitra was said to have done his sadhana before establishing the shrine of Kayavarohan.*

Amrit's longing for self-development and spiritual growth could not be fulfilled by his reading, his adventures with his friends, or by the religion into which he was born. Remembering this period he observes:

My thirst for spiritual growth could not be satisfied by following rituals that my young heart could not understand. I needed a living religion, and a living person who personified the teachings rather than just preaching about them. At the time, my entry to the inner path had to happen through a door other than the Vaishnav path. Bapuji became that door; his teachings touched my life deeply.

---

*For a more complete story on Vishwamitra and Kayavarohan, see *Light From Guru to Disciple*, Rajarshi Muni, 1974.

2·Meeting the Master

Amrit's longing and silent prayers for personal development were answered when, at age fifteen, he met the young Swami Kripalvanandji, the former Sarasvati Chandra.*

I was finding my way on the spiritual path and I would go to hear every speaker who came to Halol. One day, a friend told me, 'There is a young swami who is going to give lectures every night on the Bhagavad Gita.' I went straightaway to the place where he was lecturing, and was immediately captivated. The whole town was enamoured of this young swami. The manner in which he taught was so universal and so appealing that people of all faiths, even those who followed different religious paths, gathered around him. Shopkeepers would close their shops and children give up their play to attend his talks on the Gita. Always, 400 to 500 people attended.

The young swami was Bapuji, and when I met him that first day, I knew he was my guru. Bapuji's power as an orator, teaching through stories and parables, was totally absorbing. In those days, as a young man of 34 or 35, he was full of fire and energy. Children and old people alike would be in tears when he described something tragic and in laughter when he comically depicted human foibles. It was not just what he said, but what he was, that I recognized. When he spoke, I had an inner knowing that everything that I had been searching for in various ways could be found through this Master.

At that period I was a bold leader with my own friends, but with adults, I was extremely shy. I walked in the bazaar with my eyes on the ground and my head bowed. My father, a very powerful, athletic man, who carried a British walking stick, would remonstrate me for my extreme shyness. Yet I was so inspired to be near Bapuji that I would run to be the first one at his lectures, sitting right in front of him, very straight and very firm. Throughout his two-to-three-hour lectures, I remained still and steady, never averting my eyes from his face, never even shifting my body. I was entranced.

The town elders were privileged to fill his water glass or fan him. I ached inside to serve him in this way. Yet my shyness was too great to allow me the boldness to approach him. I desired with such an intensity to be close to him that my shyness became a real dilemma. The best I could do was go and clean the place where he lived, staying always in the background.

One day, Bapuji called me to him. He recognized something

---

*Amrit was born in the same year that the 19 year old Sarasvati Chandra met his Guru, Dadaji.

At left: Amrit at age 15 (left), with his Gurudev, His Holiness Swami Shri Kripalvanandji (Bapuji).

special in my dedication and my constancy, and in my love for him. Out of the hundreds who came daily to hear him, his attention was drawn to me. Within a few days I was able to serve him closely, fan him, stay beside him, and attend to whatever he needed. Although these privileges were reserved for the elders and I was only fifteen, I was permitted to massage Bapuji, bathe him, and attend to all his personal needs. This was the good karma that I had.

Bapuji would say things to me that indicated my future or my specialness in his eyes. One day I was massaging his feet, and he looked at me deeply and said, 'There is a very pure blood which flows in your body.' Watching me, seeing through me, he looked at me with fullest love and said, 'One day I will give you the greatest gift that you have ever received, and which you will never forget.'

Until I came to America, I waited and wondered about Bapuji's gift, hoping it would come quickly and change the course of my sadhana.

Bapuji visited Halol off and on for three years, staying several months at a time. During these times I continued to grow closer to him in service and love. With the money donated by the townspeople, Bapuji founded an organization called Gaumandir, for the purpose of worshipping cows.* In every place he spoke, Bapuji used all donations to serve the town, never keeping a rupee for himself.

Goshala was the name of a small building where Bapuji did his own sadhana; the building also housed the sacred cows. Every day, before and after school, I ran to Goshala to clean the cows, clear their stables, and serve Bapuji. His sadhana was so strenuous, with hours of yogic postures, mudras, and movement, that by evening he would be exhausted. Before his bath, I would rub Bapuji's body with a special kind of fragrant clay, which, when mixed with water, emits such a sweet smell that you almost want to eat it. I would rub this clay all over Bapuji's body and then bathe him with water drawn from the well in a bucket. I spent every free moment in Bapuji's service. When my friends came to play asking, 'Where is Amrit?' my mother would say, 'Go to Goshala. You'll find him there.' I didn't walk or run to Goshala, I floated. Afterward, when I meditated and practiced tratak (concentration exercises), I had fantastic experiences. Those were the most beautiful days, when I was a young boy with Bapuji.

At this time, I used to rise very early in the morning, about 4:00 or 4:30 a.m. and go with two or three friends to a small town gymnasium called the Alchada to work out and to practice physical exercises. There was a chart on the wall depicting asanas, and this is where I first learned hatha yoga. I didn't even know what hatha yoga and asanas were, but I taught myself all the postures from this chart and practiced them regularly. There was also some simple equipment: a single and double bar for chin-ups, some rings, and weightlifting equipment provided by the town. My friends and I worked out on these together. There were no teachers since in small Indian villages everything is very unsophisticated and unstructured, so we taught ourselves. I had been doing this for two or three years when I met my Gurudev.

One day, I was showing the postures to a small group of boys in Goshala. As I moved through the postures, Bapuji, unseen by me, came out of his meditation room and paused on the stairs to silently observe me teaching the asanas to my friends. It was not until nearly twenty years later that I learned he had seen me and that something in me had touched his mind and heart.

Bapuji later wrote about this experience:

On that day, nineteen years ago, I knew for the first time of

---

*In India cows are considered sacred and worshipped as symbols of abundance.

Top left: Bapuji outside of Goshala in Halol.
Bottom left: Amrit (directly above Bapuji in center) with Bapuji and other devotees.
Above: Bapuji at the age when Amrit met him.

Amrit's inclination for the practice of yoga. I was very much pleased with his distinctive and attractive performance of asanas. The next day, I took him upstairs to my room and gave him a personal demonstration of yogic practices. I have not allowed any of my disciples except Amrit ever to sit in my presence during sadhana, and that too, was only for fifteen minutes.

What Amrit experienced in Bapuji's meditation room made a deep impression. As he describes:

Bapuji invited me in, locked his door and entered into a deep state of meditation. His body began to move and flow in a very deep state of automatic pranic movement. The energy became so strong that his body was hurled across the room with tremendous force, dancing, moving, weaving in and out of complicated movements and asanas as I watched in awe. Being with Bapuji at that time deeply affected my life.

My later adolescence, from fifteen to eighteen, was spent in the glow of Bapuji's teachings and love. When I was eighteen, Bapuji even came to my house for dinner. I was so happy and excited. At that same time, I was approaching marriageable age. In the Indian tradition, I had been betrothed since boyhood to a little girl in my neighborhood, Urmila. She came from a very loving and spiritual family, and there was no question in my heart that I would marry her one day. According to Indian tradition, everything had been arranged by our parents, and we had never met formally or talked. But Urmila's house was only twenty yards from the place where Bapuji lectured. It was natural that she also grew to share the same deep love for Bapuji that I did.

During our betrothal, my father and mother were approached by a wealthy Bombay businessman who wanted to betroth me to his only daughter—a marriage that would have meant instant position and wealth for me, a simple Halol boy with no money. The horoscopes were matched, and a Brahmin who knew my family came and suggested this change in betrothal to us. My parents placed the decision in my hands. In my heart, I felt a loyalty to Urmila. After all our years of betrothal and the trust her family had in me, how could I cancel our commitment?

My father told me, 'Amrit, money doesn't mean everything. The culture, the heart of a person, and their spiritual qualities and upbringing are what truly matters.' I was in agreement with his advice and knew that when the time came, I would marry Urmila. I never wanted anything—wealth or position or fame—if it meant hurting someone else.

Nearing the age for marriage, I was also deepening my spiritual growth in Bapuji's service. One day he called me to him and said, 'My son, I would like to ask you not to get married for another five years.' At that time I didn't understand why he was guiding me to wait so long, five whole years. But I trusted his foresight for my life. I approached my parents and told them what Bapuji had asked of me. They understood Bapuji's purpose in guiding me to practice brahmacharya.* The next day my parents went with me to visit Bapuji. Offering their pranams, they said, 'From this day forward, we offer our son to you. Whatever you say, that is what will be done. Bapuji, Amrit is your son.'

Deeply moved, Bapuji told Amrit's parents that Amrit would reach a very high level of spiritual realization in this life. By waiting to marry and by observing brahmacharya for five years more, all of his vital energy would be focused on his spiritual growth. Bapuji taught his young disciple that when brahmacharya

---

*It is traditional in India that serious aspirants observe celibacy for varying periods of time to focus their energy on higher consciousness and sadhana.

Above: Amrit as a young man in the Indian Air Force.
Right: Amrit training in the Air Force.

is observed during youth, the body becomes like a golden vessel, full of magnetism, lucidity, and vitality. Bapuji knew that this observance would allow Amrit to direct his growth on the path of yoga.

Referring to this time of concentrated practice, Amrit recalls:

As I increased my practices and strengthened my observance of brahmacharya, my energies became extremely focused and alive. I started to develop psychic powers, such as the ability to heal people through the pulse in the navel area. If this pulse was displaced, people would have intestinal problems, weakness or even terrible pain. Simply by concentration, I could correct the pulse, and they would be instantly relieved.

At another time, I wanted to test these powers in a different way. One day, I was on the second floor porch of our house in Halol, and I saw a snake charmer on the street below. (I knew that the cobra was not poisonous. The snake charmers removed the poison sacs and teeth from their snakes.) The charmer had a flute, with two pipes that played two tunes at once. The music induced the cobra to 'dance' out of his basket. Watching him from my porch, I concentrated my energies on him and mentally affirmed, 'That flute will not play.' Suddenly the flute stopped playing! The bewildered charmer tried again and again, then looked around in confusion. Not a note would come from the flute. When I later recounted the incident to Bapuji, he told me very firmly, 'NEVER do that again.' And to this day, I've never attempted any such mind control again.

I learned from this situation not to be distracted by psychic powers and other siddhis. People become very fascinated and come to you because of the powers, but the effect is very superficial. For real transformation, the energies must be directed towards inner growth and awareness, and that is what I have done with my life.

During this period of learning with Bapuji, Amrit was also studying art with great absorption. He obtained his first job, painting "coming attractions" on movie marquees in Halol. He gave his first salary entirely to Bapuji. After that, all his paychecks went to his mother for household support; he kept no spending money for himself.

Following graduation from high school and a brief period in engineering school, which his creative nature found unsatisfying, Amrit decided to enter the Indian Air Force.

I wanted to do something unusual. I wanted to do the most amazing, outrageous thing, something that no one in my town would have thought of doing. I wanted to learn to fly, so I joined the Air Force, which is highly unusual for a Gujarati. Gujaratis are usually merchants and not physically adventurous like the Punjabis of Northern India. To travel one thousand miles away and join the Air Force was an unheard of thing in our little town.

The months of military training were a wonderful discipline for me, with my love of exercise and self-improvement. The Air Force, like all branches of the military, is a place where most young people are very distracted. At that time, I was twenty-one years old...the prime time for spending money, drinking and having fun. I never went to the movies, never took any drinks, and never ate anything other than the food provided in the mess hall. I wouldn't spent my salary for recreation but sent all my money to my family. I knew they needed every penny.

My training was going very well and I was passing all the tests with flying colors. But then I was selected for training as an Air Force gunner. I didn't want to kill anyone—just fly. I knew that a request to leave the Air Force on these grounds would be denied, particularly in view of my good record, so I

Top: Amrit on wedding day, in traditional dress.
Bottom: Amrit and Urmila on their honeymoon.

Top: Amrit in wedding procession.
Bottom: Amrit and Urmila on their honeymoon.

intentionally began to get lower and lower grades in all areas until they let me go.

After returning to Halol, I took a job teaching in the local high school. On January 29, 1955, at the age of twenty-eight, I married Urmila. As I mentioned earlier, the marriage was prearranged, and even though we had never formally met, our marriage has worked beautifully. Our love was so pure that we made all the necessary adjustments and accommodations and created a harmonious relationship. It worked, not because I pushed our marriage from an idealistic viewpoint, but because I adapted to what came into my life and because Mataji is so pure in her heart.

We are all married to life, and life does not shape itself according to our fantasies. If you can adapt and adjust to the way it is given to you, you can experience union with God.

3·Coming to America

After his marriage and a year of teaching high school in Halol, Amrit went to the Sheth C.N. School of Art in Ahmedabad to further his art training. He also took a course in Hindi Literature at the Gujarati College.

While studying at the College, Amrit heard intriguing tales of America from a close friend whose brother had emigrated to the United States. He became fascinated by stories of the land's beauty, the scientific advancement, technical achievements, and most of all, by tales of the American people's ingenuity.

Soon after receiving his diploma in art, Amrit was able to obtain a position at one of the finest secondary schools in western India, Saint Xavier's High School in Ahmedabad. There, he was able to augment his salary by working as a private tutor, since the children who attended were from wealthy families. And since the school's language of instruction was English, he was able to read more about America in journals and newspapers.

Under these circumstances, and with his customary frugality, Amrit was able to support his family and still save money for going to America. Slowly, over three years, he began to make plans for undertaking this "impossible" journey.

No one in my home town of Halol had ever emigrated to America at that time. And how was I to do this? I was only earning a bit more from private tuition than my basic salary of $30 a month. I had a wife and a young son, Pragnesh, and I had no college degrees that would allow me to get a job in America.

One day I was visiting my uncle's house and talking to him about my plans, and an astrologer was also there. He said, 'Let me see your palm,' so I showed him. After examining my palm for a time, he said, 'There is no line indicating that you will go to a foreign country.' Then I gave him my birth chart to prepare a horoscope and again he said, 'There is nothing in your stars to show that you will go to a foreign country.' I just looked at him and said simply, 'You will see that I will go.' Once I determined clearly what was right for me, I always managed to do it. I had deep inner confidence in my ability to work and to succeed.

As my plans became clearer, I consulted my mother and Urmila. I would never have gone if it would have caused disharmony for them. My mother, Bhuriben, encouraged my adventurous nature and gave me her blessings. Urmila also trusted me deeply and believed in my decision.

Of course, I also wanted to have Bapuji's permission to take this major step in my life. At that time, Bapuji had come to

At left: Amrit with his family at Bombay Airport before leaving for America. (Left to right) Amrit, Urmila, Amrit's friend Madhuvan B. Shah, his mother Bhuriben, and son Pragnesh at 6 months.

Halol again and was staying in Gaumandir. He was speaking at a special festival. There were so many people that I wasn't able to sit anywhere close to him. So I sat far away and started to silently pray from my heart, asking for his guidance. 'Bapuji,' I prayed, 'if you want me to go to America, please show me in some way.' But how could my prayer ever be answered with Bapuji so far away?

Immediately, I saw Bapuji look through the crowd right at me, and from a distance he gestured to me with his hands to go and bring him water. There were many people near him to serve him, but he pointedly asked for me to do this. In this way, I received his affirmation and the blessing for my trip to America.

Amrit sold his watch and his bicycle and borrowed money from several sources, managing to collect $600 for his plane ticket and an additional $600 for living expenses. He arrived in Philadelphia in the midst of winter, wearing a thin raincoat; he had neither boots, gloves, nor hat. Shivering in the cold, he boarded a bus to go to the house where he would be staying. The bus driver misunderstood his destination of Pine Street and let him off instead at Vine Street; his first introduction to America was walking ten blocks in the snow carrying all his worldly possessions to an unknown destination.

When I arrived, I had only one contact in this country, the names of some Indian people who were friends of my friends, and to whom I was obliged to pay rent. The American accents were difficult for me to understand, and I didn't know the customs. I was required to pay $1,000 tuition to the Philadelphia College of Art, and I had only $600 in total on which to live, eat, cover all my expenses, plus maintain my family in India. Because I was a foreign student, I was legally unable to find a job. I didn't yet know the methods for finding a job, or how to approach immigration to apply for permission to work. In addition, to receive foreign student status, I had to attend school every day and could not apply for daytime work.

Everywhere I applied for a job, I was told, 'no.' Perhaps they thought I wouldn't work well since I was a student and a foreigner and unfamiliar with American customs. Although I was a skilled artist, I was rejected everywhere. So here I was with no job, no friends, and a wife and child back in India.

In order to save money for tuition, I was hardly eating. Acquaintances noticed that I was getting very thin. I then found a job washing lunch dishes in the college dining hall in exchange for free lunches. Excitedly I wrote my mother, 'See Mama? You said I'd never be hired to even wash dishes, but here in America, I got a dishwashing job!' For several months that meal was the only one I ate each day, and I would eat as much as I could so that I wouldn't have to spend any other money on food.

Eventually, I received permission from the Immigration Department to work. Now I had permission, but no job. Since I had to attend classes full-time during the day, I had to look for second-shift work. My field was art, but art jobs are scarce on the midnight shift. I had come to America with the most expensive shoes I could get in India, but within weeks my shoes had holes in the soles from so much walking, searching for employment.

After applying for work at many factories, I got a job with a bag and paper company for $1.50 an hour on the second shift. The factory was in the worst part of Philadelphia, where there were many crimes. However, I was in ecstasy to have a job. I attended classes in the morning, and after lunch I washed dishes in the dining hall. At three o'clock I rode a bus to the factory and slept during the forty-five minute ride. I then worked from four o'clock until midnight. When my shift was finished, I walked—through the crime-ridden South Street area—to save bus fare, arriving home at about one a.m. I

Left: The first advertisement for yoga classes.
Above: Amrit demonstrating asanas in 1960 at the International Festival Ball, International House, Philadelphia.

Above: (left to right) Vasudev Rana, Dr. McCuen and Amrit during his first week in America.
Right: Amrit (standing on right) after giving first lecture to the Lion's Club in Philadelphia.

almost collapsed as soon as I got home, it was such heavy work.

Coming from India, it was a cultural adjustment to take a job of physical labor. In India, physical labor is shunned by educated people because there is always a surplus of manpower to do menial work. When I took the job washing dishes, all my conditioning came forward: 'How can you do this kind of work?' I asked myself. And then I realized that it was an opportunity to grow. I thought of Mahatma Ghandi and said to myself, 'Ghandi washed toilets, spun cotton, and swept floors for others.' All of a sudden, the energy of Mahatma Ghandi came through me. His energy started working within me, and I was completely free of cultural conditioning from that moment on.

Working in the factory was another experience. The labor union was in collusion with the management so that working conditions were unfair. My particular job was actually meant for two people, and was so strenuous that they had been unable to keep anyone on it for more than a few weeks at a time. I held that job for a year. During this period, the workers around me talked constantly about two things: sex and food. During the entire shift, this was the topic of their conversation: partying, sex, and having fun. They thought that I didn't understand English, and they made derogatory comments in my presence about my being a foreigner, which I fully understood. But I never responded or reacted. When the foreman was very strict with me, I still just accepted him because he was doing his duty.

Cleaning up the trash for the Laddie Boy Dog Food Bags was my meditation in those days. On weekends, I taught yoga classes as well as a fashion design class for the General Adult Evening School at 12th and Walnut Streets. When did I study? I didn't. I just appeared for the tests. The whole experience was a test.

Whenever Urmila hears of these days, she cries for me. But I was happy, as happy as I am now. I worked hard, and I never gave up, working to my fullest. I had such trust and faith. I knew how to conserve energy and how to survive with the minimum. It was a joy to do that. When I brushed my teeth, I would put only a little toothpaste on my brush. When I showered, I'd apply only a little bit of soap where absolutely necessary. That is the level of economy at which I lived. Yet, there was no actual difference between my level of happiness then and now. Now I have ample money for luxuries or anything I need. But to me, happiness is not that. Happiness is in my heart.

When I came, in your Western way of looking at it, I met with anything but success. I received total rejection at first from every angle. But strangely enough, I never felt rejected. There was no time for meditation or yoga. My lifestyle was a yoga: to be happy under all circumstances and to accept all that was adverse. To take life as it is: there is no yoga higher than that, and that level of acceptance is the result of practicing yoga.

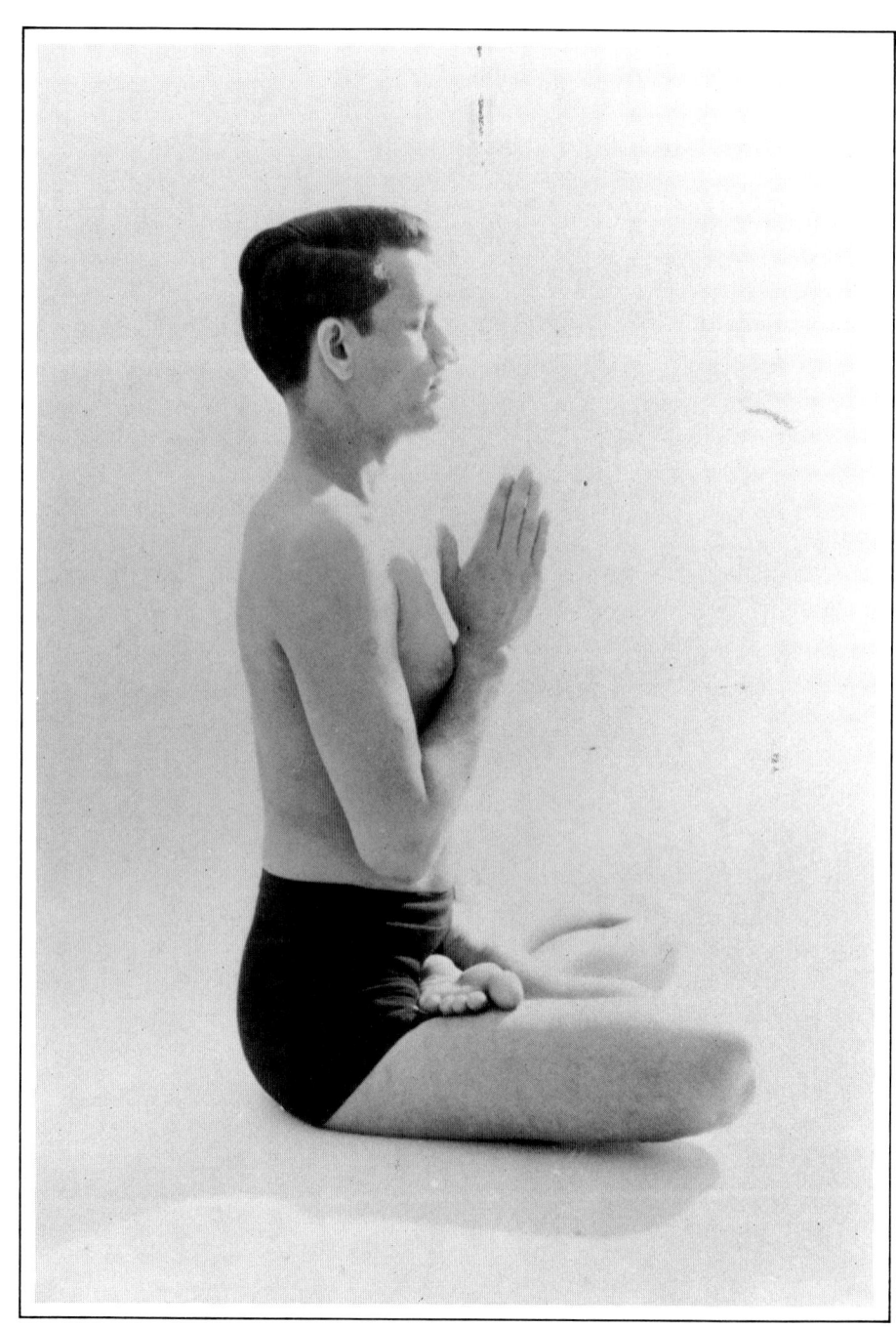

4·Discovering Kripalu Yoga

Amrit had been settled in America for only one-and-a-half years when, through his frugality and hard work, he was able to bring his wife Urmila, son Pragnesh, and younger brother Shanti to join him. It was a loving and exciting reunion as Amrit proudly welcomed his family to a land and people that he had come to understand well in a short time through many instructive experiences.

Even before the arrival of his family, Amrit had made his first presentations on yoga. He had long sensed that the real reason for his coming to America was not to practice art, but to teach yoga. Once he began teaching, he rapidly discovered a natural ability to speak about the ancient truths of India in a way that was relevant to the Western way of thinking. As a student living at the International House in Philadelphia, he was selected to represent India in a program of speakers to celebrate "International Day." Before the two thousand people who gathered for the occasion at the Bellevue-Stratford Hotel, Amrit demonstrated Hatha Yoga postures, spoke on yoga, and played traditional Indian music on his flute. Although he was untrained and inexperienced in public speaking, attending members of the media were impressed by his presentation, knowledge, and sincerity. He was then asked to appear on local television and radio shows and was interviewed by the press. Invitations followed to speak at other convention centers and festivals.

Amrit now began teaching yoga at the International House, and as a result of his frequent public appearances, he drew many students from all over Philadelphia. Urmila taught some of these classes and helped him with registration and administration. Shanti, his brother, also began to teach yoga in the area.

In 1964, Amrit graduated from the Philadelphia College of Art with a Bachelor of Arts degree in fine arts and design. During the next three years, he was employed by various design and textile firms while continuing to express his personal vision through painting. As a painter, Amrit showed great promise. His work had a certain freshness; it reflected the same nonconformity that characterized his life. Evolving through various stages of stylistic development, he exhibited his work at several galleries and art shows, receiving numerous awards and prizes. However, even while receiving recognition as an artist, the true direction of his work was becoming increasingly apparent.

The demand for his skills as a teacher of yoga was growing at a phenomenal rate. With responsibilities to his

At left: Yogi Amrit Desai meditating.

Top Left: Amrit discussing his exhibit with Kneeland McNulty, Curator of Prints and Drawings at the Philadelphia Museum of Art.
Bottom left: Amrit and Urmila at "Clothesline Art Exhibit" in Philadelphia.
Above: Amrit working on a painting for a window display at John Wanamaker's.

family increased by the birth of a second son, Malay, in November of 1962, a full-time job, and an increasing number of yoga classes, Amrit clearly was approaching yet another crossroads in his life. He was facing the choice between personal achievement and artistic recognition, on one hand, and dedication to teaching and serving on the path of yoga on the other. By 1966, Amrit had decided to dedicate himself completely to teaching yoga. Letting go of his painting and designing career without regret, he founded the Yoga Society of Pennsylvania. It was a non-profit organization providing classes for individuals interested in yoga, and training for those who wanted to become teachers.

In that same year, he made his first trip back to India since coming to America six years earlier. He took the trip primarily to be with his beloved Bapuji and to receive Bapuji's guidance for his newly chosen path in America.

Bapuji later wrote about his reunion with Amrit in India after their long separation:

In 1966, when I was in Bombay, Amrit returned from the United States. We met each other with feelings of deep affection, and he told me about his activities of yoga. During the intermediary years, he had read many volumes on Jnana Yoga, Bhakti Yoga, and related subjects. Knowing about his activities and his mentally inspired condition, my heart leapt with joy. He was initiated by me at Biwandi in the Thana district near Bombay. He then stayed with me for about a fortnight, while I taught him some techniques of yoga and gave him some knowledge of the Shastras.

Upon his return to Philadelphia, Amrit proceeded cautiously in sharing his Eastern knowledge with American students, knowing that some of the concepts might be difficult for them to integrate with Western belief systems. In those days, in the early sixties, people were embarrassed to even admit that they were studying yoga. It was very strange and new.

Amrit recalls:

When I was a yoga teacher, for a long time I was afraid to chant Om in my classes. I would justify this fear by telling myself, 'I don't want to do anything to disturb my students' faith in their own religion.' After I returned from my first trip back to India in 1966, my heart was so open from Bapuji's presence that I spontaneously began to chant Om and Ram mantras as part of my classes.

Bapuji then wrote to me, 'You must do arti in America.' I had been reluctant to do arti since it was quite unknown to Westerners, but I didn't hestitate a moment when Bapuji asked me to do it. My fears vanished because I knew that he was guiding me in the best direction. Those in my meditation groups responded positively without holding back. If my desire to serve my students had been absolutely solid at that point, I wouldn't have had any fear at all, but I still lacked total trust. I had to go through these stages of learning and growth. Every master and teacher has to go through this on one level or another.

From its beginnings in 1966, the Yoga Society of Pennsylvania grew quickly. There were soon more than one hundred and fifty classes weekly; Amrit taught twenty of these classes himself. The others were taught by teachers whom he had trained and who were sponsored by the Yoga Society. Amrit ran the Society with boundless energy, answering the phones, mimeographing newsletters, typing, cleaning, and bookkeeping. Mealtimes were constantly interrupted with telephone calls, and privacy was scarce. Urmila assisted Amrit, as did his brother Shanti. His first professional

YOGA - 'Mastery of Nature, Victory of Consciousness...'

The 'Mysteries' of a System of Self-Knowledge, Experienced by Class

By JANICE R. REEVES

Above and following page: Excerpt from an article that appeared in "The Breeze Newspaper," Nov. 22, 1962.

"Ye Gads, Yoga! . . . Standing on your head!"

When a thirty-one year old, mother of four, decides to take the plunge and take a course in Yoga, she may as well prepare herself for some eyebrow raising, snickering, surpressed grins, plus a few belly laughs.

That is, until the tormentor happens to notice a placid smile, with a "I know what you don't know, and isn't that a shame" expression beaming right back at him.

Invariably, the facade crumbles, natural curiosity breaks forth, and the most common of all questions, "What's it like?" pops out!

What IS it like? In a nutshell, it's an evening spent once a week sitting on a mat, practicing a little mental discipline, doing several non-strenuous exercises, thinking—and, you do think!, listening to the ancient wisdom given forth by your teacher, plus, as a bonus, soaking up bits of information, which when accumulated, will give you a fair knowledge of Indian Culture.

The compelling force behind all this is Amrit Desai, a handsome young man from Hald, India, who was fortunate enough to have studied under the highly advanced Yoga teacher, Swami Kripalanandji. Those of us in this course are constantly realizing that the Abington High School Directors were indeed on their toes by latching onto this deep and stimulating personality. (Incidentally, so many enrolled for the course, that the group had to be split into two classes.) At the present, students in both classes are walking about with crossed fingers, hoping that next semester, a continuing class will be added.

Come with me to a class, and see for yourself, why interest is so high.

Beginning at home, up crops the age old problem of what to wear. Being the teeth-chattering type, shorts are ruled out, so slacks, nice wooley ones, seem to be the answer. Class starts at eight, and while you zip over, you wonder if every Thursday evening will be as hectic.

Finally, the moment arrives, and there you stand, hand on the door, about to take the plunge! You yank open the door, quickly survey the scene, deposit coat, bag and shoes in a corner, then join the others sitting cross-legged on a semi-circle of mats, facing your teacher.

He too, is sitting on a mat, but n the Yoga posture known as the Lotus position (each foot, sole almost upward, is resting on the opposite thigh . . . and . . . here's an additional catch for those of you who might sit on the floor now and try it . . . the knees are not jutting out or upward, but easily resting on the floor.

The occuring thought that anyone interested in art would certainly find an interesting subject here, flashes by. For Amrit Desai possesses that classic Indian beauty of marvelous skin tone, thick jet black hair, calm dark eyes, the wide-bridged nose, and a perfectly chiseled mouth. There is no trace of tension in this person, but yet you sense a keen awareness. It is very easy for me to visualize him as a fascinating piece of sculpture.

Now, for a look around! All ages, both sexes . . . from teens, to a wonderful specimen in his seventies, who warms up before each class by dribbling a basketball around the court, leaving young men far behind, panting in his wake.

Sitting cross legged seems to produce an awful strain on snug, non-giving slacks. The other girls seem to have hit on a better solution; a., stretch pants, or b., some sort of outfit which makes the wearer look as if she had been dipped in Liquid material! Mercifully, these girls have the figure for 'em. (An inventory of one's own charms, comes out in favor of the slacks!)

For those that may be contemplating taking Yoga, you can top off slacks with a short tucked-in blouse (which comes out with every bend), or an overblouse (which has the blinding effect of obscuring your sight with every head stand).

Amrit speaks. A soft but compelling voice, welcomes everyone, and the class begins with a moment of quiet, meditation, or prayer, if you wish.

We begin a few exercises to relax. One of the most interesting observations that amazed Amrit, is the average person's inability to relax . . . and, by relax, he means completely. No tension (bodily or mentally).

Each exercise has a specific purpose, benefiting a different part of the body. For example, some massage the spine, and in doing so, provide a more supple back — a blessing to those prone to backaches. Others benefit the thyroid gland, increase circulation to the scalp (good for the hair) etc. No posture is to be done, however, with grunts, groans and quivering muscles, while ensconced in front of the television set. Don't laugh! It's been done.

Ideally, postures should be done in a quiet place, with fresh air and if possible or feasible, close to nature. Moments, in doing the exercises should be calm and almost fluid, with the body reacting instantly to the mind's wish.

Breathing also, we learn, is of vital importance. We learn to breath again . . . properly.

There's much, much more to Yoga than pure exercise, and we find our teacher a fascinating philosopher. For all of us, this is just as exciting and rewarding as reaping the benefits of the exercises themselves.

We learn it is not good to become emotional over events of which we have no control. Wouldn't it be nice not to be so emotional! I remind myself, come one of "those" days, to stop snorting fire! Wishful thinking, perhaps . . . but interesting.

This philosophy incidentally, isn't coming from a shielded recluse. No Sir! Amrit Desai lives, and lives fully.

Let's take a closer look. What we see at first is a serene Yoga teacher.

Probing beneath the surface we, not surprisingly, discover that he is a gifted artist, a musician, an art teacher, a student himself, works, lectures, and is raising a family.

Going a little further back, we discover that Amrit studied at the J.J. School of Art in Bombay, India, followed by teaching art in high school for six years and design for three years.

Arriving in the United States in 1960, he continued studying at the Museum College of Art, once again expressing an interest in fabric design.

His flair, and talent for art is very obvious to anyone who has ever had the pleasure of viewing one of his works. Currently, he is exhibiting in John Wanamaker at the World Affairs Conference and the DuPont Hotel in Wilmington Delaware. Past shows include: The Newtown Square Show (1st prize); Second Annual Brandywine Art Festival; and our local Willow Grove Clothsline Exhibit. Scheduled, and this, I feel, is a definite honor, is an exhibit the end of February, through March, at the Philadelphia Art Alliance.

Let me add, lest anyone get the wrong idea, Amrit is no frail "arty" flower . . . but a fine muscular male specimen. That the two can't mix is an all too common misconception, I'm afraid.

Both television and radio stations, too many to enumerate, have welcomed him . . . with time devoted to lectures on art, music (flute), Yoga, and India.

Schools, churches, clubs, and private groups have been intrigued by demonstrations and lectures. I had only to mention him to Mr. Harold Parachini, Headmaster of the Meadowbrook School for Boys, when an invitation was quickly extended.

secretary was a Yoga Society teacher and long-time student, Roseann Armstrong. She later shared stories of the early days with Amrit.

I remember the only time I ever heard him have doubts. I came up the steps to the Yoga Society at the house on Wayne Avenue, and he was sitting on that big stone porch being very still. I said, 'What's the matter with you?' and he said, 'Why can't I trust? Why can't I trust?' I asked him what he meant. He answered, 'Why can't I trust that God will take care of my wife and children if I give up teaching yoga classes and dedicate myself to yoga sadhana?' I loved him so much, and as I looked at him I thought, 'God love you. It's going to be okay.'

He was so neat, he drove me crazy. Everything had to be piled just so in those stacks in the office. I'm so sloppy, it was almost impossible. And still he always made me feel beautiful. I never met another human being who made me feel beautiful all the time. The first day I went to work there, at the Society, I went to replace someone who hadn't shown up, and I just stayed. When I decided to stay, Amrit sat cross-legged on my desk, and I thought, 'Where else on earth am I going to work with a boss who sits cross-legged on my desk?' He just sat there and said, 'Roseann, when you work here I want you to know that no matter what you do, I love you.' I thought, 'What's he talking about?' I feel very fortunate that he and I have been friends for a very long time. I don't have any doubts that he loves me and I never did. He loved us all with an unselfish love of caring and pure friendship. I never feel far from him, ever.

As the Yoga Society expanded and flourished, the Desai family was also growing. In March of 1968, a daughter, Yogini, was born. Amrit continued to integrate family life and service to the Yoga Society as he deepened his knowledge of yoga and shared it with his eager students.

In 1969, Amrit returned to India for intensive instruction with Bapuji. Before he left America, Amrit wrote in *Yoga Jyoti*, the Yoga Society's newsletter: "This summer our beloved Bapuji has been very kind to invite me to his ashram in spite of his own intense sadhana and has offered to teach me higher yogic practices. This call for me is like a direct call from God."

During his stay at Malav Ashram, Amrit spent six hours a day with Bapuji, learning the deeper meanings of advanced yogic practices. He later wrote of this time:

I sat at the lotus feet of Bapuji, three times a day, in the pious and peaceful surroundings, scented by the flower gardens and bathed in the fresh air. The ashram atmosphere was charged by subtle but overwhelming spiritual vibrations. I sat for hours every day and tried to quench my spiritual thirst. But Bapuji said, 'You will not understand the true value and the full significance of what you have learned until you reach these levels yourself.'

During my stay at Malav Ashram, Bapuji once mentioned to me with overwhelming love, 'It is a grace of God and divine guidance that I am opening to you the deep and hidden meanings of yoga. In the past, I have never trained any disciple so intensively, sparing six hours a day. I enjoy teaching you like I never have in the past.'

Sometimes beloved Bapuji would ask me to read from the manuscript of his book, Asana and Mudra. I often looked up as I read. Bapuji's eyes showered love on me, and I caught the glimpse of divine light emanating from his eyes. I have no words to explain these experiences. Those eyes reflected the divinity and love that he was communicating at all times. You have to see such profound spiritual love in such a saint's eyes only once to remember it for the rest of your life. I call it a sheer blessing to be fortunate enough to have had such heart-

Left: (clockwise from left) Urmila, Pragnesh, Amrit, Yogini, and Malay - 1968.
Above: (clockwise from upper left) Shanti (Amrit's brother), Amrit, Urmila, and Pragnesh - 1962.

Above: Amrit with his first car, the "old Chevy," before it was painted yellow - 1965.
Right: Urmila and Yogini - 1973.

stirring and moving moments with my Guruji.

At the time, Amrit was not consciously aware that Bapuji had given him a special blessing. During that visit, Bapuji had transferred to Amrit a measure of shaktipat (psychic, spiritual energy) in order to help him progress on the yogic path. Shortly afterwards, the grace of Bapuji's gift became an active force in Amrit's life.

It was in early 1970 that Amrit had an experience which was to transform his life and teachings: the spontaneous discovery of what he later named Kripalu Yoga. In his book, **Kripalu Yoga: Meditation in Motion,** he relates that experience:

One morning, I was performing my normal routine of yoga postures in the meditation room of my home in Philadelphia. With me were my wife, Urmila, and two of my students, John and his wife, Barbara. As was our custom, we were all greeting the dawn with stretching postures and breathing exercises.

I performed my daily routine with special concentration that morning. A tape-recording of yogic chants by Bapuji played in the background. The intonations of his voice and the gentle accompaniment of the drum stirred feelings of nostalgia and deep reverence within me. As I continued to move, I became absorbed in the rhythm of the chants. Gradually, I became more and more absorbed until I had entered a deep meditative state, even while my body continued to move. My movements had become one with the chanting.

Suddenly, as if bursting upon me like an unexpected spring downpour, I was flooded with bliss throughout my entire being, and I felt myself being irresistably drawn into another level of consciousness. As the music dissolved far into the background, I began feeling that I was no longer the performer of the exercises: they were being performed through me. A new and never-before-experienced flow of energy coursed throughout my system, and with no conscious effort on my part, my body spontaneously began to twist and turn on its own, flowing smoothly from one posture to the next. The movements were effortless and free, a command and gift from a newly opened, higher dimension of my inner being. My body became extraordinarily elastic and stretched smoothly and easily beyond its previous limits. I was not aware of giving any direction to the movements. Thoughts continued to come, but now they passed through my mind in slow motion, seemingly disconnected from my body's activity.

Although my eyes were closed, I became distinctly aware that the others in the room had silently stopped their own exercises to watch me. One after another, the postures flowed. Some of them were traditional yoga exercises; others were movements which I had never felt before. At the end of this flow of postures, my body naturally entered the lotus position, and an intense stillness, so deep that it penetrated every level of my being, emanated from within me. Suddenly, an explosion of ecstasy spread through me, and I became engulfed, overwhelmed, by a state of complete inner bliss.

About thirty minutes later, my consciousness slowly began to return to normal. With considerable effort, I was able to open my eyes, discovering to my amazement, that I was still in my own home surrounded by Urmila, Barbara, and John. It was difficult to move, and my breath was almost imperceptible. My face was completely devoid of expression, frozen, and immobile. My mouth was dry, and I realized that I had not swallowed for a long time. I tried to speak, but words would not form.

My friends mirrored my trance-like state. As I looked at their unmoving, expressionless eyes, I realized that they, too, had entered a deep state of meditation without closing their eyes. Obviously my experience had communicated itself to them without my saying a word. Gradually and with great difficulty, they began to describe what they had observed while watching me. As they slowly and quietly expressed their experience, I was amazed to hear each of them report a profound, compelling meditative experience.

Barbara spoke first. Her eyes maintained the unblinking gaze of someone who had just come out of deep meditation. In a soft, almost inaudible voice, she broke the deep silence and whispered, 'I felt as if I were doing the postures with you.'

The others nodded in confirmation. They, too, had experienced it. John spoke haltingly, 'I felt some new force take you over and begin to move your body. A brilliant light surrounded you. It was a completely new experience for me. I've never seen lights or any such phenomena before.'

Barbara and Urmila were astonished. Each of them had seen a similar bright glow during the postures. Impressed with the consistency of their reactions, I asked Urmila for her comments. Moved with deep emotion, my wife said, 'It didn't seem as if you were doing the postures. They looked so effortless, as if they were done without your control. They seemed almost— automatic.'

'Automatic?' The word rang with a sharp clarity in my mind, evoking the long-forgotten memory of the incident which occurred in India in 1950. I recalled with awe the day Bapuji had taken me into his meditation room. I remembered his remarkable yogic movements: mudras and postures, effortlessly flowing from one posture to the next with varying degrees of rhythm and tempo. Then his explanation came back to me:

'My son, all of these innumerable postures, movements and mudras which you saw me perform, occur automatically when the evolutionary energy of prana has been awakened in the body of a yogi. Yogis call this awakening of prana, "pranotthana." '

Now, twenty years later, my experience and the comments of my wife and friends brought back the memory of the incident. Was my experience similar to what I had witnessed in Bapuji's meditation room? Was it the result of the awakened pranic energy within me? This was hard for me to believe. I had always assumed that a flow of automatic body movements such as this implied an absence of all thought. Yet, I had had thoughts during my experience. Thus, I concluded that my experience could not have been the same automatic performance of exercises. And yet, what was the explanation? Intrigued, and anxious to clarify what had happened to me, I wrote to Bapuji for his interpretation and guidance. Within a few days, I received from Bapuji a typically precise and thorough answer in a neat, beautifully written letter.

'My son, your experience was indeed the result of the awakening of your pranic energy. This awakening can happen by the grace of God, guru, or through the study and practice of yogic scriptures. As a result of the awakening of the prana, the body begins to perform postures, breathing exercises, and other necessary disciplines (kriyas) spontaneously. These kriyas purify the body and mind. During your visit to India last year, I gave you special yogic practices along with specific instructions for their use. Even though these techniques were meant to awaken prana, I had withheld their purpose from you. Due to your appropriate practice of these techniques, you have been fortunate to receive the benediction of the awakening of prana, known as pranotthana.'

After this experience, Amrit began to develop a practical method to enable others at all levels of experience to enter a similar state of meditation. He began to systematize this method of "meditation in motion" so that his students could experience pranic energy and utilize it for their own healing, personal growth, and spiritual evolution. In his guru's honor, he named this approach "Kripalu Yoga."

As this higher consciousness unfolded within me, I noticed myself naturally becoming more and more loving and caring for my yoga students. My students responded to me, in turn,

Kripalu Yoga Society teachers trained by Amrit - 1970.

Above: November 1970 letter from Bapuji to Amrit, translated in part on pages 40 and 42.

At right: Amrit with Bapuji in Bapuji's meditation room at Malav Ashram.

with increased openness and shared with me that changes were being initiated in their lives also. Students who had originally begun yoga for the standard reasons—to lose weight or to learn to relax—entered into deeper, meditative aspects of Kripalu Yoga. They began to experience a renewed enthusiasm for their daily practices as I did. Their lives began to show a new dimension of peace and happiness. These changes began to appear in their caring interactions and communications with others, their creativity, and in their attitude toward their daily work.

After his deeply transforming experience of awakening and enlightenment, Amrit felt a continuing urge to begin a contemplative life. He gave up teaching some of his classes (even though it meant losing income with which to support his family) in order to devote more time to spiritual practices. In 1970, he purchased a beautiful countryside property in Sumneytown, Pennsylvania, a one-hour drive from Philadelphia. There he hoped to find a quiet retreat where he could deepen his personal sadhana. It was soon clear that events would take a different course.

Even as he left for his first summer of intensive sadhana at Sumneytown in May of 1970, many of his students came to him—first to visit and eventually to live with him and benefit from his teachings. Seeing the profound changes in his students and wanting to share his deep experiences of Kripalu Yoga with them, he turned no one away.

Following a summer of teaching these students and making the new property livable, Amrit returned to Philadelphia and the Yoga Society. Then, in November, 1970, he received a letter from Bapuji that was to permanently alter the direction of his life.

Bapuji wrote:

My son, Amrit,
Jai Bhagwan.

In my letter from Eral,* I had asked you to come here for my birthday celebration and to plan to stay with me in the ashram for five days. I am writing you the reason for this invitation now.

In ancient times the Brahmavidya,** which is known as the Yoga Vidya, was given only to the rare and most deserving disciple: to one who was not attached to worldly temptations, to one who desired only moksha (liberation), and to one who possessed divine qualities. Only he was considered to be a worthy disciple. Through his grace, the guru used to give such a worthy disciple shaktipat diksha.*** After receiving this shaktipat diksha, the disciple would start yoga sadhana automatically, and nothing had to be taught. The practice of this would lead him to the highest spiritual consciousness.

There are about five yogis in India that I know of who can give this shaktipat diksha. In foreign countries also, there are one or two Indian yogis who give yoga diksha, or shaktipat diksha. When I heard about this, I felt that it must be God's will. That is why I thought to prepare you to give this shaktipat diksha to your students so that your worthy mission will become very easy.

Give this shaktipat diksha to only two to four disciples who are not attached to worldly desires and who are of good character and conduct, so that your work will

---

*Eral—a small state ruled by a maharajah with whom Bapuji was staying

**Brahmvidya—the secret wisdom of Brahman (God)

***shaktipat diksha—This is an initiation in which the enlightened master (sadguru) causes pranic energy to awaken in a worthy disciple. That energy can transform the life of a disciple and lead him to the highest stage of yoga.

Left: Amrit meditating.
Above: Amrit doing postures.

remain alive and progress.*

When you were here last time (June 1969-September 1969) for higher training with me, I gave you only light shaktipat to help with your future progress. If I had given you powerful shaktipat, you would have often been disturbed in your present activities, and you would have suddenly left all your worldly work to go deeper into sadhana. But I did not give you this powerful shaktipat because it was my desire that you go into full sadhana only after you had organized your activities there.

This time I will seat you in front of me and will bestow upon you the yogic power to give the shaktipat diksha to others, so that this tradition may remain continuous. Remember that shaktipat does not fail even on one who cannot enter into yoga sadhana with enthusiasm and peace of mind, but such a sadhak cannot reach the highest stages.

The rest I will discuss with you in person.

Your loving Bapuji

Amrit responded with reverence and gratitude to Bapuji's invitation and returned to India. He received shaktipat diksha on January 7, 1971. Bapuji confirmed the momentous gift that he had bestowed upon Amrit with this message:

Now, after you return from India, having shaktipat diksha from me, you will be able to bring many great changes in the atmosphere of America. Whatever progress you have made in bringing the message of yoga so far was only ordinary. Now you will be able to give these higher teachings as a true representative of God. Your message will become more powerful, popular, and will be of great service to mankind.

On January 12, 1971, just as Amrit was about to leave for America, Bapuji gave him another message: it was read aloud before all the disciples at the Malav Ashram:

You have started your real yoga sadhana abroad in America, so that land has become your land of Tapascharya. Now I pray to God that one day you will return to Bharat (India), after becoming a yogi of the highest order so that I may be proud of you.

My God is not imaginary. He appears to me like you all appear to me. Then it matters little if I call that God the Truth, Brahmin, Shiva, Guru or Radha Purushottama. He is everything to me. I feel that He is more real to me than this whole world. May His grace descend upon you all, ever protect you and attract you towards Him.

With blessings, your beloved Father
Kripalu

---

* Amrit followed Bapuji's instructions and did not formally give anyone shaktipat diksha in the early years, but those who were open to his presence received the energy spontaneously when he was chanting or in a meditative state.

5·Guru and Disciple

Amrit had the opportunity to share his discovery of Kripalu Yoga with a wide audience. Invited as a guest speaker, and joining the company of such notable yogis as Swami Satchidananda and B.K.S. Iyengar, he addressed the World Conference on Scientific Yoga (New Delhi, December 1970). Following his return to America he was invited to speak to the 1971 annual meeting of the Spiritual Frontiers Fellowship in Chicago, a meeting attended by more than two thousand people. It was at this time that Amrit first saw the effects of the shakti energy that was flowing through him.

At the Spiritual Frontiers Fellowship lecture, I didn't understand how what I said could have commanded such a response from the audience. People were in tears, and many were looking as though they had been stunned. A great number told me that they had seen lights around me. I was amazed at their response.

His own path of transformation was deeply affected as well. Amrit began to have serious questions as to which direction his sadhana should take: spending hours of meditation in solitude each day as Bapuji did, or serving more outwardly in the world? Out of this period of intense questioning emerged the inner wisdom that was to make him a guru. As he recalls his experience at the time:

There was only one thing I always wanted to know about in my life. It was the one thing I would always ask astrologers when I talked with them: 'When would I begin my sadhana?'—meaning sadhana as Bapuji was practicing it. My highest realization came when I recognized that my path was already unfolding through a slightly different direction than Bapuji's. My sadhana was Kripalu Yoga, flowing with life as it manifested moment by moment. It was neither a complete renunciation nor the usual worldly life. It was a very practical method to bring the mystical experiences of meditation into daily life.

My original blissful experience of discovering Kripalu Yoga had transformed my own life, and now many were beginning to feel a similar transformation. Spirituality was no longer something that I experienced only in solitary meditation but included every activity of life. My life reflected this unique balance of living by the highest spiritual principles while fulfilling my responsibilities as a householder and an active teacher. It was a mystical journey to the state of consciousness where I was living in the world, but not being of the world.

At left: Yogi Amrit Desai.

Above: (from left to right) Amrit, B.K.S. Iyengar, Shri Kumar Swami and Shri Devendra Brahmachari at the World Conference on Scientific Yoga.
Right: Amrit giving presentation at Spiritual Frontiers Fellowship in Chicago (Rev. Rauscher, President, at right).

When I started seeing people come to the ashram, beginning in 1971, I found that my spiritual progress was happening in a unique way. I knew the principles of spiritual progress, and I looked not at the form but at the essence. The essence of spirituality is personal transformation. When I saw that this transformation was happening more effectively for me and my yoga students through selfless service, I let go of my dream of being a renunciate sadhak and gave myself fully to karma yoga.

Through helping people, the meaning of life was revealed to me. I became continuously aware of who I was. That is the tremendous power of seva. If you are objective in serving others, they become a clear, undistorted mirror for viewing yourself as you are. That's the way I saw myself; my spiritual qualities were revealed to me by my disciples.

After a second summer with students at the Sumneytown property, Amrit decided in 1972 to move his family and live there full time. In response to the request of many students, he decided to allow five men to live there and to help with the tasks of renovation.

The first person to move in was Manishi; he was the administrator of the ashram in its earliest days.

I first saw Gurudev when I walked into his hatha yoga class at the First Unitarian Church in Philadelphia. I instantly felt a special bond. It was natural that, as I worked with him, I began to question the value of my lifestyle as an architect, my relationships, my apartment, car, and career opportunities. None of these yielded the same contentment I found in my weekly yoga and meditation classes with Gurudev. When he purchased the property in Sumneytown, I thought of moving there, but still carried the fears that this opening relationship with him would, as my other relationships had, eventually prove to be not what I really wanted in life. However, I trusted him. Eventually I moved to the ashram. Growth as well as love are the hallmarks of being with Gurudev. My life with him for the last eleven years has been full of both.

Transforming the Sumneytown property into a livable home presented great challenges. The property was run down, and the main house, dating from Revolutionary days, was in need of repair, paint, and thorough cleaning. The place that was to become Amrit's home and the group's meditation center was an empty stone garage. A one-story, unheated hunting lodge without electricity stood on one hill and needed extensive remodeling. The property was the perfect training ground for the young disciples to learn discipline and selfless service through Kripalu Yoga.

Initially, Amrit intended to take only men in order to aid the practice of brahmacharya and to provide a more monastic atmosphere. But as women students also desired to deepen their study and to be nearer Amrit, he allowed Priti, and then Jyoti, Gita, and Gopi to join the small community. He guided the men and women to observe high standards of brahmacharya, as a way for them to channel all their energies into spiritual growth. In the first two and a half years, the number of residents grew from five to twenty-five, and the foundations of Kripalu Ashram were solidly established.

As a natural outgrowth of their devotion, the disciples began addressing their teacher as "Gurudev" (beloved guru) rather than Amrit. The new term communicated in a simple word the respect and love they felt so powerfully in their hearts.

The gentle guidance that Gurudev gave to the many seekers who were considering joining the Sumneytown ashram is evident in Parimala's story:

Amidst many doubts and fears, I deliberated moving into the

Above: Gurudham in the process of being remodeled.
Right: Gurudham today.

ashram. The very first time I had Gurudev's darshan alone, we sat on rocks in the garden outside his apartment. He motioned me to come closer. Of course, in my allegorical mind, I took it to mean that he wanted me to come even closer and to move in. I felt that he hardly knew anything about me, probably not even my name. As I explained my questions, he began drawing circles in the sandy soil and said to me, 'Some people just keep going round in circles looking for a solution, but then, once in a while, they're lucky to find a way out.' And while saying that, he drew a straight line right out from the circle. Though I had offered him only my doubts, in a few easy movements he gave me the answer I needed. I took his teaching to mean, 'Break out of your rut, kid; there's something else out here for you.'

Then I looked at him, and I didn't know what else to say. I couldn't explain what I was feeling, and then this mantra began spontaneously chanting itself inside my heart "I love you I love you I love you." Inside of me, it kept repeating while I fumbled around in the silence. And then Gurudev looked me square in the eye and said, 'I love you too, Jo Ann.'

Many of the students who came to Gurudev wanted to deepen their connection to the spiritual path by formalizing their relationship to him. Having read about the Indian tradition of discipleship, several of his students requested the privilege of initiation. The first initiation, held privately in Gurudev's meditation room, deepened the link between guru and disciple which had been evolving so naturally in the ashram. As more students requested discipleship, Gurudev gave the ceremony in groups—at first in groups of two or three aspirants; then in eight or ten; and within three years, for 80 to 90 at a single gathering.

Gurudev's intent in giving initiation was not to collect an impressive number of disciples, but to provide these seekers a vehicle to support and strengthen their own spiritual unfolding. The initiations were preceded by a contemplative weekend retreat which included fasting, observing silence, and reflecting on the meaning of initiation. It was a time for aspirants to open their hearts through introspection and intimate group sharing. The weekend culminated in a Sunday dawn ceremony in which Gurudev blessed the aspirants, conferred discipleship, bestowed a Sanskrit name (if desired), and formally offered the guru mantra of Kripalu: Om Namo Bhagavate Vasudevaya (I surrender to the Lord). This mantra had first been given to Bapuji by his guru, and in turn was passed to Gurudev from Bapuji at Gurudev's own initiation. Thus, Kripalu disciples were connected with an ancient lineage of teachings extending through three generations of masters, and ultimately to Lord Shiva. Their new relationship with Gurudev symbolized their deepening relationship with the divinity of their higher self.

Gurudev continually guided his young spiritual family. He worked day after day alongside his young disciples to renovate their new home: he laid carpets, poured cement, built and rebuilt, plastered and painted. In his blue jeans and bandana headband, he was as much one of them as any seeker. Yet through the example of his life and work, he was teaching them the highest principles of karma yoga.

Urmila served at Gurudev's side. Now called "Mataji," she was indeed a "Divine Mother" to the group. She often rose at 3:00 a.m. to bake fifty loaves of bread for the week. She did all of the cooking, much of the cleaning, and all of the laundry by hand, including that of the guests. Helping with the renovations, Mataji lent a strong and graceful hand in spackling, painting, and varnishing. Outdoors, the vegetable garden received the special touch of her work.

In the first year the Desai family of five shared the stone house, now called Ananda Kutir, with the five resident disciples. In the next year, they converted the garage into a small ground-floor apartment for Gurudev and his family. The apartment in "Gurudham," as the building was now called, was so small that two of the three children had to sleep in the kitchen. Above the apartment they constructed a meditation room. The new second floor was reached by wooden stairs which ran along the outside wall. The stairway was right outside the windows of Gurudev's own meditation room; all day long, he and his family would hear the noise of disciples tramping up and down. It never occurred to him to seek a more spacious and private home for himself and his family. They lived in the tiny Gurudham apartment for eight years, until they moved into a modest two-story house which the disciples had prepared for them.

Gurudev's attitude about the apartments was characteristic of his mastery of life. Although he had experienced great material success since coming to America, he did not alter his simple and moderate way of living.

I'm not going to change my standards or demands because I have become a guru. I do not increase my desires in life because I have the possibility of fulfilling them. All forms of success come to me, and I enjoy them, but they do not come to me because of my demands. If I can let them all go and be equally happy, that is the test for me of whether I possess my possessions, or whether they possess me.

Gurudev's frugality became legendary with the disciples. He saw everything—from food, furniture, and garden tools to cars, money, and use of time—as expressions of energy. He was just as creative and careful in using money and property as he was in channeling the more subtle, spiritual energies. He felt that awareness on the material plane was a reflection of a deeper awareness. A messy resident's room showed disorder in thinking; an over-furnished living space mirrored an excess of mental clutter.

Ashram residents experienced Gurudev's love for order and economy in the garden, too. Having bought just the minimum amount of seed, he would lay out rows which were precisely straight. One resident recalls how Gurudev once stopped her while she was scrubbing a metal table, teaching her how to use a smaller amount of cleanser to do the job just as effectively.

A person who sold shoes at the store where the ashram had an account remembers another story about Gurudev. The salesman recalls that, although each member of the ashram staff was allotted $25.00 to buy running shoes, Gurudev insisted on purchasing his own pair for $7.00 on sale. At another time, Gurudev bought himself a beautiful camel's hair coat for the winter. The next day, however, he returned the coat to the store. "I can't buy something for myself that my disciples can't afford to wear." he explained. Yet he never judged those disciples who were lavish in their personal spending. He simply taught them the principles of frugality; and he himself lived what he taught.

For many years, Gurudev drove an old yellow Chevrolet everywhere he went: to seminars, lectures, and business meetings. The disciples tried in vain to have him purchase something worthy of his position and more comfortable for his many long trips. But he wouldn't hear of a new car until a resident, who borrowed the vehicle for ashram errands, accidently wrecked it beyond repair.

Top left: Early group portrait of Gurudev, Mataji and residents.
Bottom left: Early group photo of a few ashram residents in Sumneytown.
Above: Gurudev leading renunciation ceremony.

Above: Mataji working in the garden with residents.
Top right: Gurudev with Yogini.
Bottom right: Gurudev and Manishi studying architectural plans for the ashram.

Although the residents sometimes joked about such frugality, the lessons in conserving energy went deep, affecting not only their purchasing habits and possessions but their use of time and of creative and intellectual energy as well. Residents learned first-hand that a simple item, carefully purchased, well used, and treated with awareness, yielded more satisfaction than a multitude of hastily acquired possessions. In this way, Gurudev established the basis for the entire ashram's use of time, money, energy, and materials.

In the early years, the young Western disciples had many such practical lessons to learn. Their vision of spiritual life did not include dishwashing, cleaning, and ditchdigging. Meals, prepared and served by Mataji, usually culminated in long periods of drinking tea around the dining room table while Mataji washed the dishes and Gurudev carried lumber or paint through the room on the way to the next task.

Saturdays were "karma yoga days," when Mataji and Gurudev asked the community to share in the work. Gita, one of the first women to join the ashram community, recalls how the residents responded to the concept of a "karma yoga day":

Gurudev and Mataji would make a list of all the things to be done, and we were supposed to volunteer for projects. At that time, we had about fifteen residents and hadn't yet organized the seva. Mataji would start to read off the list. She would say, 'Weed the garden?' and look around. Everyone would look out the window. Then she'd read, 'Help in the kitchen?' and everyone would look blank. So then Gurudev would begin to teach us about karma yoga—never judging, but teaching and helping us understand. Some Saturdays he would teach for two to three hours about what karma yoga was and why we should do it to grow spiritually. Our awareness was not very high.

Vinit, another member of the ashram community, shared his recollections of Gurudev's teaching about seva.

Gurudev was always teaching us by setting an example. At one time he was showing me how to paint, something that I didn't do very well. My paint kept on dripping, so Gurudev would take the brush and say, 'First time just put on a little bit. Then, with the second stroke put on more, and it will go on smoothly.' His part always looked great, but when I tried to copy it, I couldn't do as well. I knew he wasn't attached to my doing it a certain way, but I would get frustrated with the way the job was turning out. Finally I said to Gurudev, 'I'm going to take a break,' and he said, 'Don't give up. It will get better.' He always saw how beautiful something could be, and if people were working with energy and enthusiasm, he'd be happy.

He would teach us in satsanga, and then follow up with a group project to keep the energy high. If people started spacing out and taking too many tea breaks, he wouldn't order us back to work. Sometimes he would come in and just start doing the work himself, inspiring us with his own enthusiasm. That's how he used to motivate us. He was a very patient perfectionist.

Through his own hard-working example and many hours of teaching, Gurudev patiently showed his students the principles of karma yoga.

I guided the students by accepting wherever they were and taught them by the example of my own life. I did not operate from an idealistic or moralistic view of life, but from one of love, dedication, and service.

When people came to the ashram, they came with a spiritual dream. They thought 'spiritual' meant meditating all the time, not taking any worldly or financial responsibility, having a healthy diet, and living in the woods. They didn't want to get involved in anything which demanded responsibility of them;

they thought that was 'unspiritual.' Their attitude was, 'If you're meditating, that's spiritual. If you're working, that's work.'

To help my disciples move into a yogic approach to life, I taught them constantly and extended continuous love and acceptance of what they were feeling and going through. I never pushed them or blamed them. I let them understand that spiritual life is not just ideal 'spiritual values,' but means taking responsibility. I had to teach them how yoga spreads into your entire life; everything that you do becomes spiritual. Spirituality is nothing less than taking an active role in transforming your energies in every expression of life.

The power of Gurudev's presence is that he is not merely communicating ideas through speech; he is communicating truth through his entire being. His speech, actions, gestures, how he chooses his priorities, the way he spends his time—all aspects of his lifestyle are working together to make a harmonious statement of the essence of spiritual life.

This was true in the early days of the ashram as well as now. Gurudev's daily schedule from those early days through the present would stagger the mind of a busy executive. His day often begins as early as 6:00 a.m., with personal writing or with teaching small groups. Through the gatherings with special groups such as married disciples, senior disciples, and new residents, he maintains and strengthens strong personal contact with his large spiritual family.

Early morning darshans are usually followed by a series of meetings with residents for conducting ashram business and for counseling. Flowing from one need to the next with intuitive insight and mental acuity, Gurudev may work with an architectural team, giving input on the designs for building renovations; meet with the financial controller to encourage better uses of ashram funds among the department coordinators; then see a visiting Kripalu Center leader from Canada who is dealing with group conflicts and leadership questions. His greatest delight is to give highly creative solutions to challenges of using time, money, and energy. A resident struggling with questions of career-versus-ashram life might be next, hoping to find clarity in the unbiased perceptions of his teacher.

In the early afternoon, Gurudev's secretary often has to remind him that it's an hour past his lunchtime. He laughs, startled to discover the time. After eating silently by himself, he continues meetings into the late afternoon or early evening. Those who go for darshan enter into an atmosphere saturated with peaceful vibrations of love and harmony, an environment reflecting order and beauty, sweet with the scent of incense. No one leaves Gurudev's presence untouched by the experience of his love and insight.

At the end of the day, Gurudev sometimes continues in meetings and counseling right up to evening satsanga. At other times, he has dinner with his wife and children, even as eager residents and guests fill the meditation room, waiting to be in his presence.

During these long days, Gurudev rarely experiences any tension. Always in the flow of the moment, without expectations of the next person or event to come into his life, he maintains a flexibility which makes each moment new and absorbing. Entering satsanga smiling and radiant, he is ready to lead the group in chanting and dancing. Then he settles into an inspired discourse or a spontaneous interchange, to hear people share their experiences or to answer questions from the group. What happens is totally unpredictable and surprisingly well-suited to the needs of those assembled. A fortunate guest

1974 resident portrait with (center) Mataji, Gurudev, and Gurudev's friend Ghanshyam Shah from Bombay India.

or disciple who desires some extra personal contact might be invited to walk him home, so that even in the last moments of the long day, Gurudev is listening, teaching, loving—pouring his life into those who gather to be with him.

From the earliest days of the ashram, Gurudev has consistently given his time and energy to help his disciples grow and learn. When the community was young, he spent much of his time counseling residents individually about their day-to-day conflicts, questions and concerns—situations which involved, for example, jobs, relationships with parents, health, shakti experiences, and adjustment to ashram living. As the community matured and older residents absorbed his teachings more fully, he shared the counseling duties with them. This step allowed Gurudev to turn to a deeper level of teaching and a more creative role in the development of the ashram.

This story of Jyoti's illustrates the way in which Gurudev persevered in helping the disciples through his acceptance and firm, but loving, teaching.

In my early years at the ashram, I went through a lot of growing pain. All of my self-images were breaking down, and none of my expectations of myself were being met. I had thought I was going to be a saint, and I kept finding all sorts of faults: jealousy, anger, blocked emotion, and fear. I was very frightened. I would ongoingly seek comfort, solace, and guidance from Gurudev. He was always there, very much like a mother to me. He would always love me, allow me to cry, gently hold my head, and constantly tell me I was okay. While I judged my neediness and hated myself because I thought I would never change, he responded to my deeper need to be heard and my child-like need to be loved.

At one point, I was struggling so much with my fears that I went into the mountains and camped out all alone, then spent a weekend in silent retreat in the ashram. After some time in retreat, processing my emotional needs, I had come to a feeling of greater peace. I stopped by Gurudham to deliver a letter I had written to Gurudev. I wanted him to know I was fine, trusting the process and working on myself. As I entered the house, he called me into his darshan room. The sun was streaming in through the door making a golden pool of light on the moss green rug. Gurudev's favorite scent filled the spotless simple room. Gurudev was seated on the couch. He looked at me with a glance so piercing that I squinted the same way I would in the noon day sun.

'How was your retreat?' he asked.

I began to speak, telling him of some of my deep realizations. Then he stopped me and began teaching. He leaned forward towards me, and speaking directly in a strong, clear voice:

'You say you have faith, but you continue to worry and fear and allow yourself to get stuck in your emotions. Trust in God means you really give up the fear. Trust means you are no longer dependent on external sources for love. All those securities are temporary. Give love, don't drain it from others. Give understanding.

'How long do you want to stay stuck? I'm not impatient. I'll be helping you forever; all of this lifetime, or however many lifetimes it takes. But it's your choice! How long do you want to be in it? You have to make a firm decision to work with what's happening in your sadhana; to trust; to be really fearless.'

I felt Gurudev's power and love being aimed at me like pointed arrows. I felt his words enter deeply into my heart, my body, and my mind.

Even as he spoke, I realized the transforming power of the truth in his teachings. I experienced the laser beam of his love directed at me, changing the whole make-up of my body-mind. In spite of his directness, he was infinitely tender. He reached for me like a mother reaching for her child, and suddenly I put

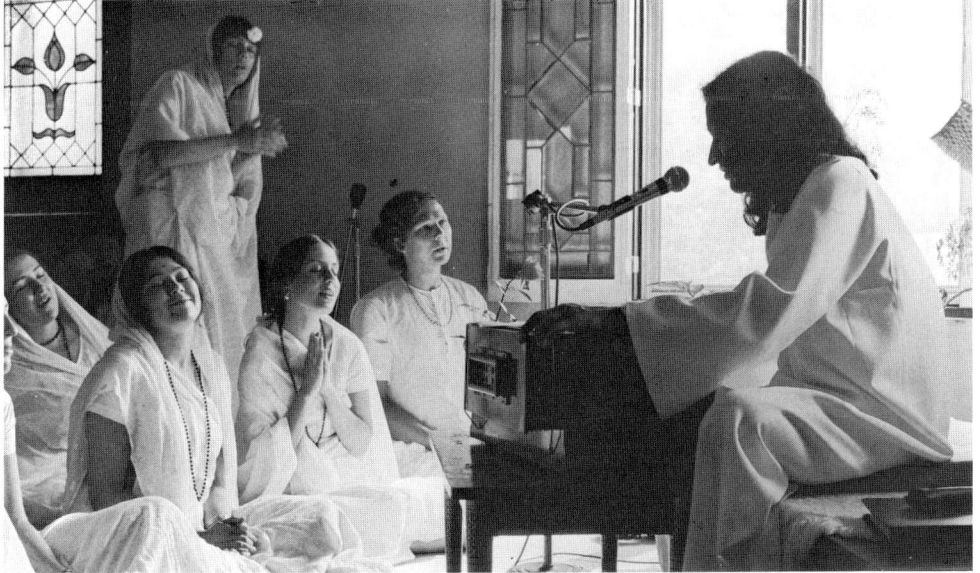

Top left and right: Gurudev and disciple at Kripalu Retreat (Summit Station).
Bottom: Gurudev in satsang at Kripalu Ashram (Sumneytown).

Above: Gurudev with disciples at New Jersey beach.
Top right: Gurudev leading postures at Ursinus College retreat - 1975.
Bottom right: Gurudev leading morning jogging.

my head in his lap. He was stroking my hair and wiping away my tears, softly telling me, 'Always remember, I love you.'

To a master such as Gurudev, the difficulties experienced in life are not problems solved with "shoulds"; rather, they are vehicles for the disciple's spiritual growth. While always straightforward in his teaching, Gurudev would still respond to individuals in particularly appropriate ways. The same question might be presented to him by ten different people, and he would respond in ten different ways. Some would be mothered and reassured; some challenged; some given a specific practice to work with; some gently rebuked or scolded. Gurudev's guidance for disciples who had developed a good measure of self-awareness and trust, and who had integrated his teachings into their belief systems, provided them with a penetrating insight into themselves.

While totally accepting the uniqueness of each disciple's growth process, Gurudev never compromised his principles. It was important to him to maintain the high standards of spiritual life and to take care that the teachings of yoga were not diluted. A particular challenge came in teaching the principles of brahmacharya, as he shares:

The early '70's were the height of 'new age' values: lots of hugging, being 'mellow' and not taking responsibility. I had a hard time at first, sharing the teachings of higher spiritual life, particularly with the practice of brahmacharya.

It was very difficult to establish the practice because the young people who came to me did not come from any specific religious direction. They were not looking for in-depth spiritual disciplines like a person who was entering a monastery. Many of them were trying to escape from life's challenges without being aware of it. Others were looking for a natural 'high.'

When the time came in 1973 for me to establish permanent guidelines about brahmacharya and celibate living, it was really difficult for many people who were accustomed to touching and hugging as expressions of love. But no matter how much time and effort it took to guide the disciples, it was never a burden. My love for them gave me acceptance, and helping them gave me continuous energy.

As Gurudev poured his energy into the disciples, teaching them about ashram life, and, as many received shakti experiences, the devotion and dedication increased. The hearts of the disciples opened through the experiences of shaktipat, and the relationship of guru and disciple emerged spontaneously without the disciples having any formal knowledge of the Indian tradition. Standing when he entered and left the room, dressing in white clothing for satsang, bringing him flowers and fruit, and bowing at satsang naturally emerged in the lives of the disciples as their love intensified. With such adulation, it would have been difficult for many teachers to maintain their selfless sense of service and their humility. However, with his natural modesty and his grounding in the guidance of Bapuji, it was not Gurudev's need to become a guru. He simply adapted to the changes in his life as they occurred, never losing his sense of purpose.

He recently shared the inner wisdom that guided him:

I have no problem of attachment to any of my disciples, or any need for them to act in a certain way towards me. If I had attachment, I wouldn't be able to do justice to the truth. Truth is whatever is needed by a disciple to help with their inner growth. If I had a need for them to love me, recognize me, or respect me, or any need to seek their approval, I wouldn't be able to help them. As I have expanded my nonattachment, I have also expanded my capacity to truly love.

I had planted a seed of consciousness in those early years. Everything you see blooming today in the ashram was in a seed form in those days. Because I accepted the seed and nourished it, it has blossomed. I didn't feel any differently when the plant was only a seed than I feel today when it is flowering. I accepted the disciples exactly as they were on a very realistic plane. I always stayed in the moment.

6·Channeling the Energy

The high spiritual energy generated by Gurudev's presence was deepening and expanding the experience of ashram life. Side-by-side with the practical lessons he was teaching his disciples, the energy of shakti flowing spontaneously through him created an atmosphere of intense devotion for God and guru.

Throughout 1973 and 1974, seminars and satsangas with him were infused with deep, meditative experiences of this shakti, or divine energy. In his presence, or through his chanting, many underwent powerful cathartic experiences and spontaneous kriyas. The release of emotional and physical blocks was accompanied by sounds, movements, spontaneous chanting or dancing, and other experiences. The flow of shakti, which happened naturally and without conscious effort on the part of Gurudev, opened even deeper feelings of love in the disciples. It also brought about tremendous changes that accelerated the transformation and purification processes. As more people were touched by the flow of shaktipat through Gurudev and found their lives being deeply changed by his teachings and unconditional love, he was invited to give seminars on yoga and spiritual growth all over Canada and the United States. Colleges and universities were often the sites of his seminars, with as many as several hundred people attending at a time. Everywhere he spoke and chanted, people experienced spontaneous kriyas—life-changing releases of blocked energy—and profound moments of feeling God's light came flooding into their being.

Vidya, former director of the Syracuse Kripalu Center and a six-year resident at the Kripalu Yoga Ashram, shares her experience of meeting Gurudev during this period:

Finding a 'guru' was the last thing I had on my mind when I first met Gurudev. My purpose for being at the 1973 Yoga Convocation at Watson Homestead, New York was simply to hear the teachings of the many guest speakers who would be there. An intellectual frame of reference was what I was looking for, a place to ground my burgeoning interest in my spiritual development. I didn't know at the time that true spiritual teachings and the messenger must be one. I was soon to find out.

On the second day there, while eating lunch, a newly arrived group was ushered into the cafeteria. They were not specially introduced nor given particular attention, so I assumed there was nothing noteworthy about them. I had barely swallowed my next bite when my eyes fell on one member of the

At left: Gurudev in a meditative state during which many people experienced spontaneous shaktipat.

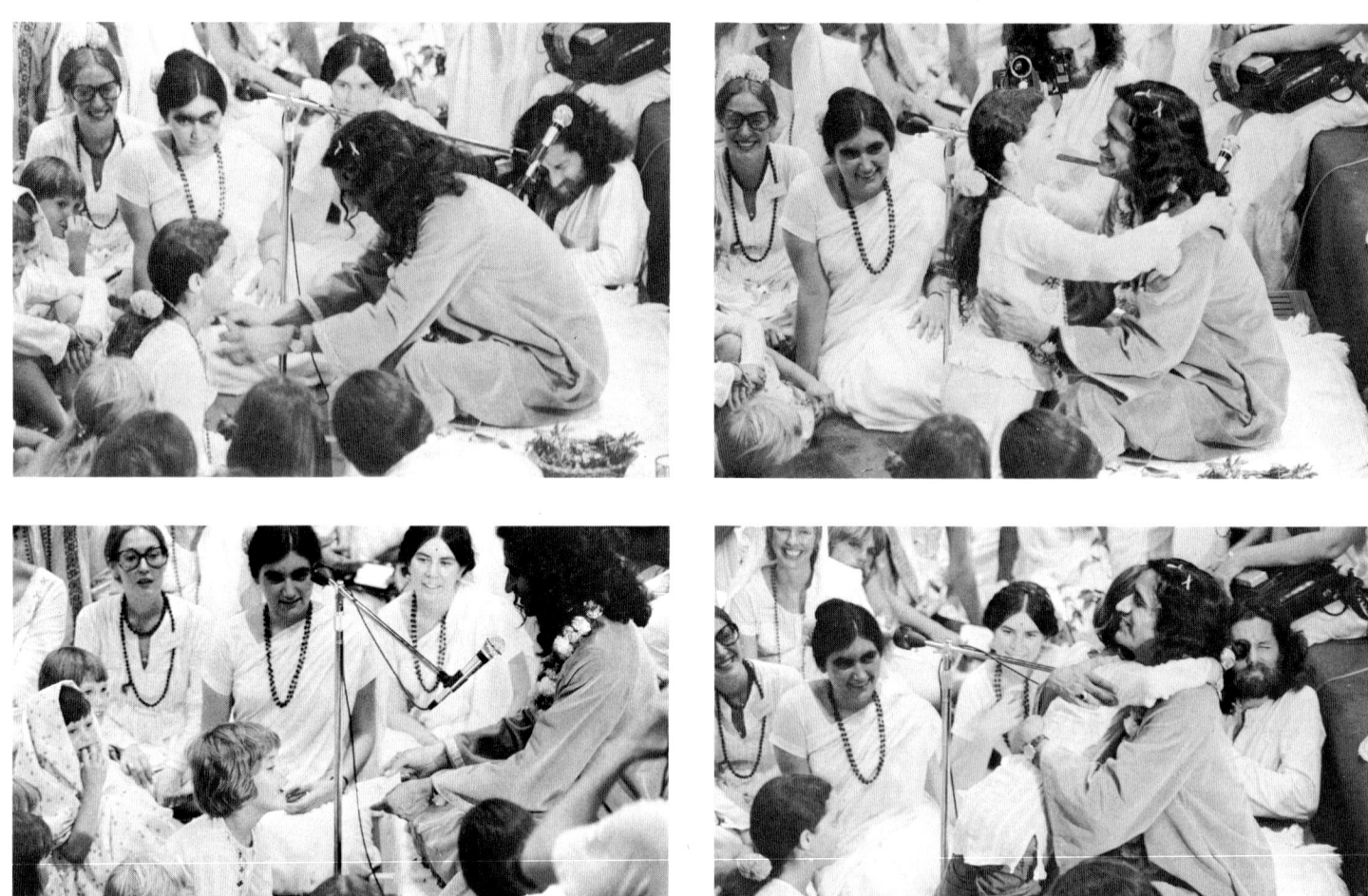

Gurudev with children at satsang.

group standing conspicuously in my view. I looked, and looked again. Tears slowly filled my eyes. The tall, lean figure of a man sharp in features and princely in stature plummeted my awareness away from myself and into my 'center.' The man with long, dark hair that now stood before me had the same face, eyes and features as that of a face that had appeared in a dream two months previously.

Like the offspring forever tied to its parent though the cord has long been broken, I felt deeply connected to this man. I had no idea who he was, whether teacher, speaker, or simple seeker like myself. Standing before me was a being radiating peace and light. Though there was a great distance between us, the humility and gentleness so obviously a part of him were as tangible as the white clothes he wore. My quiet tears soon became convulsive weeping as every cell of my body was overtaken by the almost painful ecstacy of being united with a long lost, sacred part of myself. Nothing mattered in the moment, no food, no talk, no quizzical comment that my mind could make. Only my heart could verify this experience. I was seeing with eyes I had never used before, while my senses were enraptured in the visible realities of that moment. It was my soul, long awaiting its entrance into my conscious life, that recognized this man as the being who would give it birth, who would set me walking on my way to God. My teacher stood before me.

Like a child who naturally runs to its mother after long separation, I found myself walking over to Gurudev. When I reached his table, I bent down and heard myself say, 'Thank you for coming.' The words meant more than a mere salutation. I was feeling the speechless experience of being captured by an energy far greater than my mortal self.

Undisturbed by my coming to his side, Gurudev's eyes welcomed me. His gentle hand reached out, and stroking my head, he closed his eyes. For a few silent eternal moments we shared the awesome joy of the meeting of guru and disciple.

Our eyes opened in unison, and before me was the radiance of divine love shining on his face.

A journalist attending the 1973 Watson Homestead Conference described his first meeting with Gurudev in an article entitled "Instant Cosmic Consciousness?"*

The first thing I noticed was a wave of euphoria softly permeating my being. I felt intensely happy. I didn't know the reason for the wonderful feeling, but I was determined to relax and enjoy it.

Suddenly surges of energy—like electrical charges—streaked up my spine. These gradually evolved into a steady current of hot energy flowing from the tip of my spine to the top of my head. My impulse was to analyze intellectually what was happening, but I quickly realized that the more I thought about it, the less I felt it. So I stopped thinking and concentrated on experiencing.

Brilliant colors swirled inside my head; I thought I would burst with happiness. Nothing ever had felt so good! Suddenly a scream burst from someone in the back of the room, then another. In a few moments the place was a madhouse. People were crying hysterically, laughing uncontrollably, gasping for breath, even rolling on the floor. Apparently everyone was experiencing some manifestation of the same energy I was feeling.

...My body filled with a brilliant white light, and I allowed myself to be absorbed in it. I felt that my life, as I previously had known it, literally came to an end. My ego identity became meaningless; there was no time; past and future did not exist. All that existed was pure light and pure bliss. I was content to remain in this state forever.

---

*John White,(ed.), *Kundalini, Evolution and Enlightment*, Anchor Press, 1979, pp. 184-188.

When I opened my eyes again, I noticed that my body had bent forward: my forehead was touching the floor. I do not remember assuming that position. I was actually bowing down to Yogi Desai. I had never bowed to anyone in my life, but some inner unknown force had prompted me. I knew I wasn't bowing to Amrit Desai, but rather to my own higher self which he had helped me to see.

He was surrounded by persons who, only hours before, had never seen him but now sat on the floor around him weeping unashamedly. Men and women of all ages and professions had found a part of themselves they never knew existed. I knew those people were feeling love and bliss and that Amrit himself was without ego. After a lifetime of practicing intense yogic disciplines, he knew he was only a channel for transmitting the energy the others experienced.

The leader of the Watertown Center, Gayatri, also connected with Gurudev in an intense exchange of energy.

I first met Yogi Amrit Desai in 1971 at St. Lawrence University before I was 'ready.' His lectures, meditations and explanation of postures were all beautifully direct, and yet what I remember most was his honesty. After the lecture, in my first personal encounter with him, I asked if he knew about Kriya Yoga, a path which I'd heard could speed up one's growth. Since I wanted enlightenment in six months or less, I was anxious to receive kriya initiation.

Yogi Desai smiled politely and in a rather shy way admitted that he did indeed know about Kriya Yoga and that one must have a teacher in order to practice it. I immediately offered all the reasons why this wouldn't be possible for me: children, distance, husband, family, household duties, etc.

He simply stated, 'That's okay. When you are ready, the teacher will appear.'

I remember feeling dismissed, and yet I recognized the simple truth of his forthrightness. This was just a small preview of a later learning that evolved during our relationship: Gurudev cannot and will not be manipulated. He loves everyone and sees our best and our worst qualities, but he is free of judgment because he needs no one's approval.

In spite of my unmet expectations, I persevered and went to several lectures that Gurudev gave. In January of 1973, he came back to St. Lawrence University and demonstrated the meditative posture flow of Kripalu Yoga. I was caught by the natural flow and grace of his movement which was so spontaneous and free. Parts of my body responded and relaxed as he flexed the corresponding areas of his body in the automatic flow of asanas. The whole group was very quiet and still. Afterwards when he sat in meditation, he suddenly started with a sharp intake of breath. His head seemed to snap back. At literally the same instant, I felt vibrations like pins and needles in my arms, then a cold trickling feeling like water running down my arms—much the same as when a nerve has been touched. This feeling continued well into the evening.

When I asked Gurudev about it, he said it was a shakti transfer of energy. He called it shaktipat, energy passed from guru to disciple.

I had many other experiences of shaktipat through Gurudev after that. I began to understand what he had told me in our first meeting about the need for a teacher. How comforting to have a guide to help confront the fears; he was someone who had traveled on the road before, and I felt his deep love and acceptance of all that was going on inside of me.

Many at St. Lawrence University, and at other conferences, received the shaktipat and divine love of Gurudev. The hundreds of letters that Gurudev received after his seminars made it apparent that people's transformative experiences were profound and powerful,

At right: Gurudev demonstrating a Kripalu Yoga posture flow.

Above: Gurudev in a meditative state during which many people experienced spontaneous shaktipat.
Right: Woman experiencing shaktipat.

as illustrated in the following excerpts:

You led us into meditation and began to direct the energy through our bodies and through our chakras. I could see the energy rising up through my body as though I were an observer... I was looking down and through my body. I could see the centers becoming more and more active, growing and pulsating, but then I lost the sight. I became enveloped in light.

The energy pulled my body into a sitting position with no effort on my part. My hands put themselves on my knees in a final surrender. My personality disappeared. You came over and touched my forehead, and it felt as if the touch went through my head. The light and love and truth touched my very essence. It was like a shock shooting through me. There was no separation with anything. Love was bright and truth was all.
—Washington, D.C.

My head and palms swelled with energy and light. It seemed as though I was an awareness of energy and light, not in my body but above it. Before coming out of this state, I remember visiting my heart center. There I heard a rumble. The longer I listened, the clearer the rumble became. Soon the noise became a sound—the sound of music. It was deep, monastic voices chanting 'Om Namo Bhagavate Vasudevaya.'* I was certain that the song was, and always will be, sung in my heart.
—Syracuse, N.Y.

Listening to the chanting, I was wafted up and up on your current of devotion. I saw flashing colors behind my closed eyes: orange, blue and a brilliant, calm green. Also, I saw many ever-changing mosaic patterns, all exquisitely intricate. Sometimes my breathing became very regular, and at other times it grew forceful. I began to notice that no matter where my body was in space, my center was not moving but remained completely still! At those beautiful times the physical world would retreat for a few seconds. My arms kept reaching for the sun, floating up like growing plants.

Suddenly the rocking motion of my body seemed to correspond to the rolling gait of a huge animal as though I were riding an elephant. The image was of being in a joyous procession of many people I love. We were all riding and singing in great happiness with flutes playing and finger cymbals ringing. We were on our way to some long-awaited place or state. The bond of love I felt between us was incredible. I can hardly describe the beauty of the scene. It glowed and sparkled like a perfect jewel.
—Columbus, Ohio

Many who received the grace of shaktipat established a close link with Gurudev; they integrated the changes in consciousness they were experiencing into their lives, often intensifying their spiritual practices. Yet others found the psychic energy too powerful to be productively channeled and utilized in their daily lives. Some people experienced difficulty in reconciling the internal changes they were feeling with their past lifestyles and established patterns of belief.

Gurudev spent much of his personal time counseling and guiding the disciples through this period. He came to the conclusion that some changes would have to be made in directing this energy to disciples and other followers. As he related:

I eventually stopped the intensive outward flow of the shakti energy because so many were not ready to handle the intensity of the physical, mental, and emotional purification that it brings. If you cannot purify your communications with others and in your daily life, how can you purify on a spiritual level?

---

*The mantra given by Gurudev at initiation.

Top left: Gurudev with Swami Shri Satchidananda.
Bottom left: Gurudev with Yogini, Murlidas and Sant Keshavadas.
Top right: Gurudev with Swami Shri Rudrananda.
Bottom right: Gurudev with Swami Shri Muktananda.

I realized that my disciples needed more grounding, more clarity in their thoughts and emotions, and more purification in their bodies before moving to this deeper level. Bapuji was realizing similar things in his work in India and at that time wrote to me: 'Do not give shaktipat except to a few ready disciples.' I had come to the same conclusion. Yet, at any time, the shakti can flow. When I go very deeply into meditation or spontaneous chanting with a group of people, this often happens. People who love me and are open sometimes have shakti experiences in my presence. The energy flow is not stopped; it has become more subtle.

Kripalu Yoga was the perfect replacement for these shakti experiences for my disciples. With shaktipat, they had been moving into a complete surrender to prana without any control from the mind, and it was too intense for them. With Kripalu Yoga the energy is awakened and surrendered to, yet the mind is conscious and in harmony with prana. It is the perfect balance between willful practice and a sadhana of complete surrender. I consciously introduced Kripalu Yoga to my disciples as a channel for this energy.

The power of Gurudev's presence brought many people to visit Kripalu Ashram. Between 1973 and 1975 there were few structured programs for guests, but Gurudev was continually in residence and gave lengthy satsangs on weekend mornings. Among the guests who visited the ashram were many Indian and American spiritual leaders. The ashram was honored by a visit from Swami Shri Chinmayananda. Swami Shri Rudrananda (Rudi), a noted karma yogi, came and taught disciples about the disciplines of selfless service. Sant Keshavadas was a frequent guest as well and taught the ashram disciples chanting and skills in Indian music. Sri Vasudevadas, of Prama Dharmasala in Virginia, trained children's program staff in spiritual approaches to child care. Dr. Mishra of Ananda Ashram in New York became a friend of Gurudev's and came often to the ashram. Swami Shri Sivananda Radha from Canada and Yogi Bhajan of the 3HO Organization were others who exchanged visits with Gurudev. At this time Gurudev also made the acquaintance of Srila Prabhupada, the founder of the Hare Krishna movement, a man who Bapuji held in great respect for his selfless work in America. The ashram disciples benefited greatly from these visits with noted spiritual teachers and enjoyed learning how others presented the ancient teachings to Westerners. Visiting speakers had nothing but the highest praise for the disciples, the ashram and, above all, Gurudev.

Whenever he was on a speaking tour, Gurudev visited as many spiritual centers as possible, absorbing all that he could to help the Kripalu organization. Among his contacts were Baba Free John of the California Dawn Horse Communion; Stephen Gaskin at The Farm in Tennessee; Philip Kapleau at the Zen Center in Rochester, New York; Swami Shri Kriyananda at Ananda Ashram, California; Baker Roshi at Tassajara Zen Center in Big Sur; Swami Shri Rama of the Himalayan Institute in Pennsylvania; and Swami Shri Muktananda at his New York ashram. Always open and receptive, Gurudev learned from other teacher's approaches to inner growth. He brought his experiences back home to share them with his disciples and to integrate them into his own practical approach to personal development.

In 1973, Gurudev felt the inner yearning for a period of sustained silence and meditation, to deepen his own sadhana and to give him a still more intensified experience of the ancient practices of yoga. He decided to spend a three-month period in total seclusion. The disciples responded with heart-felt support, knowing that

Above: Gurudev coming out of seclusion, 1974.
Top right: Muktidham.
Bottom right: Gurudev with Mataji and disciples, after he came out of seclusion.

the spiritual work Gurudev carried on would affect their growth as much as his own. They enthusiastically designed a beautiful, but unpretentious meditation home to be built high on a hill in the forest overlooking the Sumneytown ashram. Working hard throughout the fall and early winter of 1973, the residents pooled their skills, labor, and love in constructing the building for Gurudev's sadhana.

Gurudev had planned to enter seclusion on December 9, 1973. Since it became clear that the dwelling would not be finished at that time, he began his seclusion in the meditation room of his small apartment. From this retreat, he sent frequent written messages of inspiration and guidance to the ashram disciples, encouraging and teaching them as they lived without his daily presence.

On January 27, 1974, in the middle of the night, Guruji quietly relocated and settled into the completed house, naming it Muktidham, or Home of Liberation. The same day, he wrote a letter of love and encouragement to his ashram disciples.

My Beloved Disciples. Jai Bhagwan.

I am pleased to see you all doing so well. Even though I am not with you physically, I very much feel the harmonious vibrations. Everyone seems to be doing well, but there is always room for greater awareness and improvements. At times some of you may go through the high and low periods; this is natural. Do not take it seriously, just watch it pass by. Always maintain equanimity, balance and harmony.

My love is equally available to all of you. I love each one of you. Each one of you is a link in a chain. This chain which is my support in my steep climbing is no stronger than its weakest link. It is the duty of each one of you to take every opportunity to help your brother or sister who is in need and keep the chain strong and together through love and service to each other.

Once you have come to me and have become a link in the chain, it automatically becomes my responsibility as well as that of the other links to see to the well-being and strength of each link.

Your strength is your peace and love; preserve and help reserve (it) at all times.

Today when I arrived here at Muktidham I felt that this is not just a building but a monument of love. That is the way Muktidham (The Abode of Liberation) should be. I was taken by surprise to see love and beauty everywhere I looked. Everything is done so precisely well. The altar is a masterpiece. I do not know how to thank you all, those who have worked hard and poured their heart to make Muktidham possible. I have seen you work day and night.

There is so much beauty combined with simplicity of design that I kept on looking every part of Muktidham over and over. This really shows what love can do! This is not just love to talk about, but an active love.

My sadhana is progressing well with the blessings of beloved Gurudev. * *It is a very, very auspicious sign to have rain at the time I entered seclusion December 9th and also today when I was moving to Muktidham.*

My divine children, continue to grow in love, selfless service and surrender.

With Love & Blessings
Yours, Amrit
Jai Bhagwan
Om Shanti

The seclusion was a time of heightened spiritual awareness for guru and disciples alike. One of the first experiences Gurudev had was the eradication of a childhood fear which he had carried into adulthood. As

---

*Bapuji

he relates:

From my childhood I had a fear of being alone in the dark, where there were no people to help me in case I was in trouble. When I was very little, my whole family would be sitting in one room, and if my father told me, 'Go check the attic door and close it,' I couldn't say no to him, yet I would be so afraid. I'd climb into the attic, and quickly push my head in and look all around fearfully, so no one lurking up there could hurt me. Until I went into seclusion in Muktidham I carried this fear, but was never in a situation to allow it to surface and be worked out. Suddenly, there I was, all alone in the woods, and this same fear came along my first night. I became very focused on it, and said to myself, 'In all these years, how often have I felt this fear, and known that it never became a reality?' Instantly, with this realization, I decided not to think these fearful thoughts, and it never once came up for me again. I dropped it then and there and went right to sleep. God gave me life. He can take it in the way He wants to take it.

The three-month seclusion was a landmark both for guru and disciples. For the first time, the ashram residents had to function without the guiding presence of Gurudev, making administrative decisions, maintaining the guidelines, and working out interpersonal and personal difficulties according to the teachings they had absorbed from him. Gurudev's seclusion was a training period in which disciples took on the work and responsibilities that he previously had been handling himself. A maturing process took place which would allow Gurudev more time and freedom for teaching, personal sadhana, and spiritual work. In addition, the disciplines of morning practices, karma yoga, evening satsanga, and brahmacharya became firmly secured in the daily life of the ashram.

With the maturing of the disciples' ability to manage the ashram came a new challenge. Following his seclusion, Gurudev took fifteen of the disciples for a three week visit to India, leaving the remaining residents to administer the ashram on their own.

The May 1974 pilgrimage was an extraordinary event for both guru and disciples. The apex of Bapuji's work in India, the construction of a magnificent temple at Kayavarohan, had been completed. There was a huge celebration to dedicate the temple and install within it the sacred lingam which carries the image of Bapuji's guru, Bhagwan Lakulish. More than 50,000 devotees from all over India came to take part in the ceremony. Gurudev and his disciples, seated in the front of the large crowd, were among the special guests. Gurudev delivered a speech to the large audience, paying homage to Bapuji and his service in creating the temple as a universal pilgrimage center.

During the same trip to India, Gurudev was honored by the Shankaracharya, one of the four highest spiritual leaders of Hinduism in India. On May 11, 1974, at his ashram in Dakor, His Holiness Jagadguru Shankaracharya Maharaj conferred the degree of Doctor of Yoga Science upon Yogi Amrit Desai. Few degrees of this nature had ever been conferred by the Shankaracharya.

The effects of the Indian pilgrimage extended throughout the Sumneytown ashram. The contact with Bapuji and their spiritual lineage in Kayavarohan inspired the disciples in a deep way. Having learned about Indian arts, rituals, and the ways of honoring the guru, they incorporated these customs into the community's spiritual observances. The quality of devotion in the ashram grew steadily, infusing the daily life of the residents with a deepening commitment to their spiritual path.

Above: Gurudev receives "Doctorate of Yoga" from His Holiness Jagadguru Shankaracharya in India.
Bottom: Gurudev with Swami Shri Chinmayananda at Sumneytown ashram.

In the spring and summer of 1974, the ashram took a great leap in expansion; twenty new residents arrived, enlarging the community to more than forty-five. A new resident dormitory, designed and built by the disciples, was opened in July of that year. More programs were provided for the increasing numbers of guests who wanted to be near Gurudev, receive his teachings, and spend time in the peaceful solitude and loving atmosphere of the Sumneytown ashram. Gurudev expressed the purpose and attraction of the community in the following way:

The purpose of the ashram is to give you the groundwork to unfold your higher potentials through helping others. In the process of serving, the ashram is naturally going to expand. It is not my intention to expand purely for the sake of growth. The expansion comes because of the stage of sadhana of my disciples. They need to serve in order to integrate the teachings more deeply in their lives.

In early 1974, we had a waiting list for residency, prior to the opening of our new dormitory, Guru Kripa (Guru's Grace). Up to that point, I personally owned the ashram and everything in it. I saw that my personal profit was going to increase dramatically as large numbers of people came to live here or to attend programs. I didn't want to a be a businessman and involve my energies in moneymaking. I wanted to use the income to benefit more and more people. Shankar, Krishnapriya and I got together, and I told them that I wanted to turn the whole organization into a non-profit group that would benefit the work.* Then I handed over the entire organization to the Kripalu Yoga Fellowship. I relinquished all personal profit, and simply took a yearly salary to support my family and myself.

The Kripalu Yoga Fellowship soon mushroomed with tremendous growth. Disciples were living three per room and in an apartment rented in the local town. Guests attending weekend programs were housed in every available nook and cranny, while disciples often moved out of their own rooms to provide adequate space for the visitors.

With such overcrowded conditions, it was soon imperative to find some growing space. In 1975, a second ashram, Kripalu Yoga Retreat, was purchased in Summit Station, Pennsylvania.

The new 250-acre summer resort came complete with three-acre lake and twelve run-down but usable buildings—an answer to a dream. Within a year of purchase, a huge dining and dormitory complex had been built, other buildings renovated, and a smooth-flowing ashram community was in operation. The effort needed to accomplish such a great work in such a short time showed the results of Gurudev's teachings of directed, purposeful service.

Six months after the move to the new Kripalu Yoga Retreat, the disciples were putting on ten-day sadhana retreats, month-long teacher training programs, and relationships workshops. The combined population of both ashrams had swelled to over two hundred residents and included a large print shop and publications department as well as departments in architecture, kitchen administration, accounting, child care, housekeeping, maintenance, and a curriculum library for Gurudev's tapes and transcripts. The residents actualized Gurudev's teachings day by day through the practice of

---

*Krishnapriya (Sandra Healy) is the director of Kripalu Yoga Ashram and Retreat, and secretary to Gurudev. Shankar (Michael Risen) is the director of his own actuarial firm and a close disciple of Gurudev's. He has served on the Kripalu Yoga Fellowship Administrative Board since 1974.

Above: The Retreat property at present.
Bottom: Satsang during construction of the Retreat chapel.

karma yoga—working together, resolving interpersonal conflicts, meeting individual needs, and discovering the joy of serving others with love. As the disciples expressed the love and service which Gurudev inspired, Kripalu Yoga Retreat began making its mark in the Western spiritual world.

7·Bapuji in America

For many years, Gurudev had been inviting Bapuji to come to America. During each trip to India, Gurudev told Bapuji how suitable the American ashram would be for his sadhana; he described the quiet atmosphere, the freedom Bapuji would have from worldly demands, the devotion of the Western disciples and their longing to serve him. Yet, knowing that in twenty-eight years Bapuji had not once altered his daily sadhana, Gurudev had only a faint hope that Bapuji might actually come to America before achieving his complete and final samadhi.

During a visit to India with some of his disciples in 1976, Gurudev again petitioned Bapuji with deep conviction, saying:

Bapuji, you must come, not for any other purpose but to do your sadhana. It will be so convenient for you to do your meditation in America. We have Muktidham, a meditation house in a secluded woods on the top of a small mountain where you will not be disturbed.

Still, Bapuji told Gurudev, "Not yet."
Then one day, Gurudev was sitting with his master. Bapuji looked very cheerful, and said:

Today I have good news. I will come to America. But remember, I am not coming as a missionary, to change people, or to spread my teachings. I'm not coming for money or fame, or to increase my circle of disciples. I'm not coming simply to be with my grandchildren. I'm coming because of your love.

In the middle of a winter night in early 1977, Krishnapriya received a long distance phone call: Gurudev was calling from India with the news that Bapuji would arrive in three months. Calling around the ashram in the middle of the night and awakening the disciples, she excitedly shared the news, "Bapuji's coming!"

"Right," responded one sleepy and unbelieving disciple, "and when is Dadaji coming?"

Gurudev returned home for a brief period to guide the disciples in making the preparations which would be important for welcoming Bapuji. The ashram residents worked day and night to prepare homes for Bapuji at both the Ashram and Retreat. It was decided that Bapuji would spend the fall and winter at Muktidham in the Sumneytown ashram, and would move to the Retreat in the summer. An old concrete block building at the Retreat was completely transformed into "Rajeshvari" (a

At left: Mataji (fourth from left), Roop Verma, Bapuji, Shri Krishna Shankara Shastriji and Gurudev in a procession.

Above: Gurudev translating Bapuji's message at John F. Kennedy Airport after his arrival in New York.
Right: Bapuji at Kripalu Yoga Retreat.

home for a king).

During this time, Gurudev taught the disciples how to prepare their hearts as well as the ashram to receive Bapuji. He asked them to chant japa, in shifts, all around the clock to purify their consciousness and attune themselves on subtle planes to Bapuji's highly evolved state. Gurudev explained:

Bapuji is such a being that it is very difficult for the mind, or the usual consciousness, to comprehend his magnitude. Externally, he appears to live a regular life. He eats ordinary food, and when necessary, he discusses administrative matters related to his humanitarian work in India.

Yet he is a saint. He is one of the greatest living masters on this earth. Everyone feels that about their guru, but Bapuji has demonstrated this. He has shown an exquisite degree of tolerance, patience, and perseverance in his search for God. He has meditated ten hours a day, and has maintained complete silence for twelve of those years. Since 1971, he has spoken only on rare occasions when he addressed large groups during sacred celebrations.

Our ability to experience Bapuji is directly proportional to the teachings that we have digested. I want each one of you to increase your capacity to absorb our master while he is with us. Nothing is more powerful for increasing your capacity than love.

What do I mean when I say "love"? Love means total openness and receptivity without imposing any of your expectations. To receive from a master, you must be totally still inside. If you meet Bapuji with tension and expectations, you will not meet the master; you will only meet your fears and expectations. Bapuji will disappear. To go for the darshan of a saint or master, you must go empty and humble so that he can fill your cup. If received properly, Bapuji can transform your life.

You all must have truly prayed for Bapuji's visit. No one in India could believe that he is actually coming. This is the wonder that love can perform.

Gurudev returned to India in order to accompany Bapuji on his journey. Then, after months of preparation came the beautiful spring morning in May 1977 when Bapuji arrived in America. Speaking to the ecstatic disciples at Kripalu Retreat, Bapuji said:

My beloved children, there was absolutely no possibility of my coming to America. And yet, I have come, drawn by your pure love. It is well known that a magnet has the power to attract iron. You are all magnets of love, and you have attracted me here. I have not come here to propagate yoga or religion or meditation. I have simply come to greet you.

What an amazing happening this is. Where is India, and where is America? Truly, love knows no distinction between countries, dress, appearance, virtue, or age. I have a firm and complete faith that your pure love will be of great help to me in completing my sadhana. As your spiritual grandfather, my blessing is that this entire group of seekers may go all the way to the gates of God.

When Bapuji first arrived, he had kept almost total silence for eighteen years. Yet, when he felt the openness and devotion of his Western "spiritual grandchildren," who had yearned for so long to receive his teachings, his loving heart opened still wider. He spoke to the ashram disciples and guests every morning, beginning the day at 6 a.m. with chanting and then teaching them for more than an hour at a time. Then he resumed his silence and seclusion. These darshans were a magnificent gift, intended to inspire and last in the hearts of the disciples for a lifetime.*

During these early morning hours with Bapuji, the chapel seemed infused with light, with magic. Bapuji's chanting, his inimitable storytelling with his dramatic gestures of pathos and comedy, the unconditional love that showered from him, touched the resident disciples and guests in ways they would never forget. At Bapuji's feet always, translating, serving him water, fanning him and adoring him, was his disciple Gurudev. In Bapuji's presence, Gurudev was transformed into childlike purity, completely focused on his master, and ready to serve his slightest wish. He was totally intent on creating the most appropriate surroundings to protect Bapuji's sadhana.

There was a new depth in the close personal contact between Bapuji and his most devoted disciple. Gurudev protected Bapuji from all external activities such as the many requests for him to teach or to meet important guests. He was also careful not to impose any demands on him, so that Bapuji always felt free and comfortable to follow the daily routine of sadhana and writing to which he had dedicated himself.

Mataji also served Bapuji with a constant love, never missing a day as she prepared beautiful meals for him and looked after his housekeeping needs. Her entire day was organized to serve Bapuji. She made sure that she was never late with his meals, knowing how punctual and precise he was in his sadhana. Bapuji allowed her to serve very closely and regarded her as his spiritual daughter. She, in turn, copied down everything that Bapuji wrote on his slate, keeping the treasured words like scriptures in her personal diary. As she served him, she became soft and radiant, suffused with a joy and a light that was noticeable to all who knew her well.

Bapuji originally intended to stay in America for only nine months. However, the devoted service of Gurudev and Mataji, the love of the disciples, and the peaceful setting for his sadhana drew him to extend his visit longer and longer, to the delight of his Western family.

By October of 1977, five months after his arrival, Bapuji had settled into Muktidham to resume his meditation and silence. With the exception of two yearly speeches, he gave only one darshan a week for the remainder of his four and a quarter years in America. He came to the Sumneytown meditation room every Sunday precisely at 3:15 p.m. for a brief darshan with ashram residents and visiting guests, sometimes delighting them by writing a brief parable on his slate.

As Bapuji's sadhana progressed, Gurudev shared with the disciples more about his relationship with his master.

Bapuji is extremely blissful. You can see the joy on his face. He is sweet—so sweet. Today I was telling him, 'Bapuji, I'm so glad you have graced me with the blessing of your being here.' I had tears in my eyes. I could feel how deeply he took in my love as he bent over and patted my head. Then I told him, 'I just don't know how to express my gratitude to you. You have showered such grace upon me that you are doing your sadhana here.' Then I filled up with tears completely and could say nothing more. To me, this is the experience of infinite love with a master. Unless you first feel like father and son, which is one of the deepest loves, how can you move further into a guru-disciple relationship?

Bapuji's love is so all encompassing, that no matter what I do, and no matter what he knows of me, he accepts me. When you feel this way with me, you know now where the love is truly coming from. I have dedicated everything in my life to

---

*These lectures have been printed in Pilgrimage of Love, Books I & II, by Swami Shri Kripalvanandji.

Top Left: Bapuji telling a story while Gurudev translates.
Bottom Left: Bapuji teaching while Gurudev translates at Kripalu Yoga Retreat.
Above: Bapuji blessing disciples while Gurudev and Mataji fan him.

Gurudev, Bapuji's disciple.

Bapuji, and I want nothing more than to serve him. When I sit with Bapuji, I become like a four-year-old. I can't be any other way with him. During the 1974 trip to India with ashram disciples, they all noticed this and commented to me, 'Gurudev, you look just like a little boy when you're with Bapuji.'

How many people on this earth can have such a relationship as we share with Bapuji? Who would take you on such a basis of unconditional love? Where could you go to express and experience love like this? This is the essence of the guru-disciple relationship—where you can sit and be innocent like a child and know you will be taken care of and protected, and nourished and guided and loved?

Bapuji's love for Gurudev, his spiritual son, was equally deep. At his 1981 birthday celebration, the last he was to celebrate, Bapuji had this to say of his devoted disciple:

I have been considering beloved Amrit as my son from his very childhood. The feelings of being a guru and the feelings of being a disciple are revealed from the heart. Those feelings can never be forced. I naturally feel that Amrit is my son and that he is my disciple. I am satisfied that he has served me to the best of his capacity. It is but natural, being father, that I should give some advice and inspiration to him to help him advance.

Bapuji's encouragement for Gurudev took many practical forms. As well as teaching him and giving him the tremendous gift of shaktipat diksha, Bapuji conferred on him the title of "Yogi" in 1969, at a ceremony in Kayavarohan, where Bapuji was Chancellor. The title was given in recognition of "significant knowledge and practice of the principles of yoga."

Later, in 1980 during the Guru Purnima celebration in America and before a gathering of hundreds, Bapuji awarded him the title of Yogacharya (Spiritual Preceptor). The award recognized Gurudev's "years of intensive study, teaching, and practice of the philosophy and spiritual principles of yoga." It also honored his selfless dedication and service to humanity, and his development of the unique theory and system of Kripalu Yoga.

Soon after this occasion, Bapuji's guidance to Gurudev took a new turn. He requested that Gurudev make a pilgrimage alone to India, encouraging his disciple's natural humility and simplicity.

Bapuji wrote on his slate during an ashram darshan:

I have advised Amrit to go to India and live for a while with saints. By doing this he will receive new light. I also have given him a hint, a piece of instruction. I said, 'My son, do not go with the label of "yogi." If possible, go as a common person, a person who is willing to learn. Inside of yourself, be aware that you are a yogi.' My purpose in sending him to India is that he move and live with the great saints, learning from them and putting their teachings into his life. I sincerely desire that Amrit's travel is successful, and that all of you will also receive the benefits.

Gurudev traveled to India as Bapuji suggested in the winter of 1980-81, dressed anonymously and going as an ordinary seeker to visit many great saints and ashrams. When he returned, he shared fascinating stories of his travels and the great teachers that he had encountered. But the deepest change was subtle, one that came through his awareness and touched everyone in an undefinable way.

Bapuji gave what was to be his last long discourse to a Western audience during the Guru Purnima in the summer of 1981. Those who gathered to receive his darshan were moved by the depth of love emanating from him. Many disciples at the ashram sensed that a major change was occurring for Bapuji. In mid-September, a special darshan with him was arranged at the Kripalu Retreat. Disciples from all over North America and Canada were contacted and invited to be present. All sensed that he might be leaving. Gurudev was self-contained and quiet, more attentive than ever to Bapuji's needs. Bapuji had become increasingly weak and his health had declined over the past year; he walked to darshans with great difficulty and effort. He was barely able to take food due to the intensity of kriyas and purification processes taking place in his body.

On September 27, 1981, Bapuji gave his final darshan to a large crowd of loving and tearful disciples. His brief message, inscribed on his slate and translated by Gurudev, was etched in the hearts of all his spiritual children:

Beloved children, Jai Bhagwan with love.

I came here to America solely for the purpose of meeting you all, and I imagined that I would stay here for only nine months. But today, four-and-a-quarter years have passed. I have stayed here longer than I had anticipated. During my stay here, I have had the good fortune of bathing in the lake of your love and drinking its waters daily. I have felt these four-and-a-quarter years to be like four-and-a-quarter days. I have always experienced happiness with your selfless service. With the grace of God, I have not found any flaws in that service. I consider the collective love of every one of you as the love of the Lord Himself. For me, it is a divine gift of love.

I have always considered Amrit as my own son. During my stay here, for four-and-a-quarter years, he has never displeased me. He has loved me for many years with faith, and I have also loved him deeply. His pure love is one of my sources of satisfaction. Urmila has also served me with love. There has never been any ebb in her enthusiasm.

Today the long and sweet dream of four-and-a-quarter years has come to an end. On the Guru Purnima celebration, I had declared that I would be going into seclusion. According to that decision, I am going into more restricted seclusion. I beg your permission to say farewell. I belong to the Lord, and I sincerely pray that I will always belong to Him.

Beloved children, do not give up virtuous conduct and self-discipline, even in the face of death. Keep unflinching faith in the holy lotus feet of the Lord and continue practicing mantra japa, bhajans, chanting His name, meditation, pranayama, postures, observing holy vows, fasting, moderation in diet, studying scriptures, and other disciplines. I extend my blessings to everyone.

Your loving Grandfather,
Kripalu

Although Bapuji made no mention of returning to India in his message, many disciples felt that he would soon return to his beloved native country. Within a week, it was announced that Bapuji quietly had departed for India with Gurudev. When Gurudev came back from India, he announced that Bapuji was staying with loving disciples in a secluded place and was being cared for with great devotion. Although transcontinental communication with India was always difficult, Gurudev kept in close touch with the disciples who were taking care of Bapuji.

On Tuesday, December 29, 1981, at 6:10 p.m. in Ahmedabad, Gujarat, Bapuji passed peacefully into Mahasamadhi, leaving behind his body as he underwent the final liberation of a great master. As soon as Gurudev received the message, he called together the disciples. After chanting prayers and having a brief meditation, he

Above: Bhumi Pujan, a special ceremony performed by Bapuji. (right to left): Shri Krishna Shankar Shastriji, Haren Dave (a Brahmin priest), Bapuji, Mataji and Gurudev.
Left: Bapuji in a Guru Purnima procession.

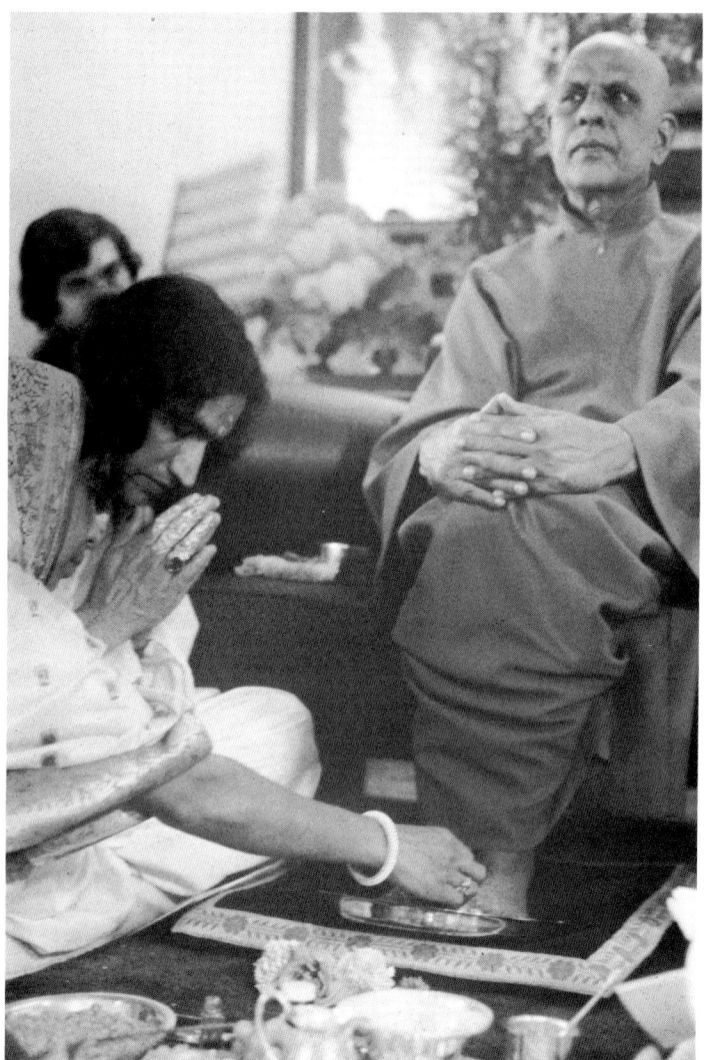

Above: Mataji and Gurudev performing puja to Bapuji.
Top right: Mataji serving Bapuji his meal.
Bottom right: Gurudev bowing to Bapuji after demonstrating a Kripalu Yoga posture flow for him in the presence of disciples.

spoke.

This morning I have called you for a very important message. I wanted to be with you, and for us all to be together as a family, to share this with you. Bapuji has taken Mahasamadhi. I had a letter from Bapuji recently in which he said that the path of yoga is facing death at any moment. But such a death of a master is not death at all. The master, Bapuji, does not live in the body. As you all know, in the last one-and-a-half years Bapuji has been going through the experience of being unable to eat. Yet he would not take vitamins, special foods, or medical treatment. Bapuji said to me, 'No matter what is happening to my body, I have to go through it in whatever way it happens.' He knew that his body was merely a vehicle. He had a complete trust in God, and whatever came, he took it as the grace of God, all the way to the end. Bapuji has not departed from us. He is such a great master that he is more among us now than ever before.

I invoke the presence of our beloved Bapuji. May he envelop each one of us with his energy of love. May he give each one of us his guidance for carrying on the divine work which he has initiated. May he permanently establish his presence on the altar of our hearts. We know, beloved Bapuji, that you lived to love God and nothing else. You loved us as your children and grandchildren, and when you came here, you broke your silence out of love for us. We need your strength, your love, and your life to guide us in your footsteps. Come, Bapuji, let your life, your dedication, your joy, your love for God and for humanity shine through each one of us so we may continue to carry the torch of love as you did all your life.

Beloved Dadaji and Bapuji, give us the strength and courage to face this life in dedication to God, to guru and to all humanity. Give us strength to let go of pettiness, selfishness and fears to become true channels of love. Give us the awareness to keep before us the message of your life, a guiding light for each of us.

Let us envelop our Bapuji with love. Know that this love is the love of God and Dadaji coming through us. Om Namo Bhagavate Vasudevaya.

The love and prayers of the Kripalu family followed Gurudev back to India, as he went to say his final goodby to the body of his beloved master. At the Sumneytown ashram, the women residents joined Mataji in doing continual japa around the clock. Taking turns, they continued japa until the day of the Indian ceremony celebrating the soul's liberation, sixteen days after Bapuji's death. This celebration coincided with the anniversary of his seventieth birthday. Before an altar that held Bapuji's shoes, slate and pen, festive with candles and incense, Mataji led the assembled women disciples in chanting and bhajans into the early hours of the morning.

The days of Bapuji's residence at the ashram were over in a physical sense, but his spirit continued to shine more brightly in his family's heart than ever before. Bapuji had left his body but not his grandchildren. His dharma of love and truth, carried through Gurudev, Mataji and the disciples, would keep expanding in the deeply transformative, loving, and conscious service of the center that carried his name: Kripalu, the Compassionate One.

8·The Path of Selfless Service

The years that Gurudev and the disciples shared in loving and serving Bapuji strengthened the foundations of ashram life and became the basis for extending the teachings of Kripalu Yoga on an international level. Gurudev has emerged as the beloved leader of a large spiritual growth center which is attracting people from all over North America and much of Europe. His disciples are now teaching and serving as many as several hundred guests each month. Living in the presence of a master and learning from his life, the disciples have come far in realizing their potential for giving. Like rough diamonds they have been polished to reflect his light.

With unwavering patience, Gurudev has taught the disciples how to serve, how to give, and how to love the many guests who come for programs, visits and retreats. The disciples see people from all walks of life, many of whom come with great difficulties—struggles with their health, relationships, or finances. There are others who bring with them only the desire to grow spiritually. Again and again, Gurudev receives each person with total acceptance, never measuring their lives by a philosophical or moralistic yardstick. His most effective tool is his ability to consistently love and accept everyone, even as he helps them to work through their problems and uncover their higher potentials.

When Gurudev counsels residents and guests in satsangs, he is a model of acceptance and love. He uses each situation as an opportunity to train the disciples in counseling through his example. Even in the presence of the most disparaging or highly emotional guests, Gurudev remains calm and loving, encouraging their full expression without judging them. Sometimes the disciples react to a particular guest, thinking, "Gurudev will never tolerate this," only to be taught another lesson in acceptance and understanding.

One incident, recalled by a senior disciple, illustrates this point:

In 1977 a woman with a strong personality was a new guest at Kripalu. She asked very pointed questions in satsang and around the ashram. Many of us felt disturbed by her manner. She challenged our values of celibacy and modesty, and her endless questioning about the ashram had a defiant tone. Several residents with counseling experience in the ashram made written recommendations to Gurudev and his administrative assistant that we ask her to leave, something that was very rarely done. Gurudev's response was to call together all counseling and teaching staff for a special darshan.

At left: Gurudev teaching at Shadowbrook in Massachusetts.

Gurudev teaching.

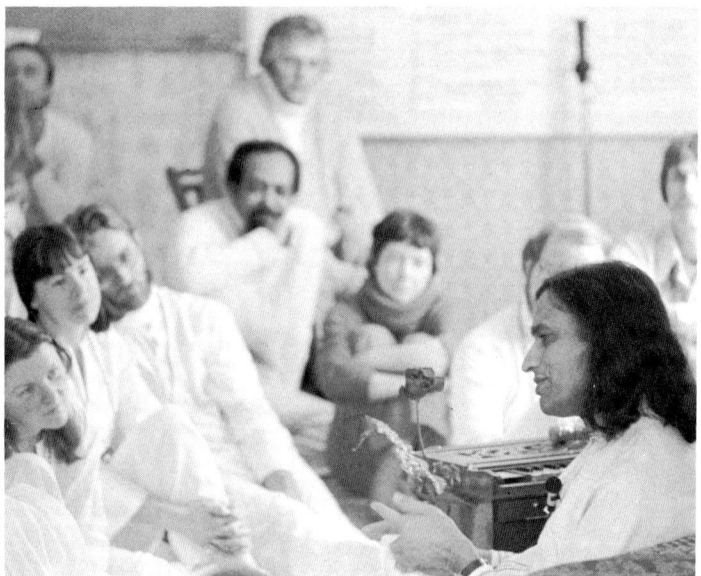

He taught us about serving our guests and looking on them with compassion and understanding. He showed us that the ashram existed to help people with their lives, and to give a basis of spiritual love and support for those in need. He made it clear that he wanted our guests to feel accepted, loved, and understood for who and what they were at the time. This did not mean that we had to reinforce their negativity, but they were to be helpfully guided toward new understanding.

He then talked about this particular woman, and taught us to observe the way in which he had repeatedly counseled her:

'I listened to all of her questions without evaluating her on the basis of her fears. When I worked with this difficult woman, if I had been stuck in the fear of my own personality, I would have been caught up in that aspect of her problems, guilt, or fears and I would have gotten everyone else stuck when I answered her. By answering her in a nonattached, nonjudgmental way, I am revealing her to herself and allowing us all to learn from her growth.'

Then he asked us all a question that left a deep impression: 'Where else can people go for the acceptance they need, if not here? If we judge and turn away, where else can they find love?'

As always, he taught us patiently. Where we had seen defiance, he had seen need; where we had seen an obtrusive, imposing personality, he had seen a seeker whose quest for truth was so strong that everything had to be challenged. It was a profound lesson in the way we were to serve others.

This woman eventually moved into the ashram and lived with us for a year. She underwent tremendous personal change, becoming a very peaceful and loving person—a welcomed part of our family.

Gurudev began training the disciples to teach the Yoga Teachers Training Program in 1974. He felt that yoga teachers were diluting the message of yoga by concentrating on weight reduction, tension relief, and physical improvement. As he saw it, the concern of the yoga teacher could be no less than a deep interest in personal transformation. When the teachers found fulfillment in their own lives through inner growth and health, they would naturally be dedicated to sharing their experience.

While training the disciples as teachers, Gurudev worked with them closely, showing them how to serve the guests on a deeper level. These teachings were to become the basis for all Kripalu programs:

I teach the ashram teachers that in whatever program they are giving, the technical knowledge is not the most important element. The most crucial part is the student-teachers' love for their personal inner growth. What they in turn give to their clients is more of an outpouring of what they have learned— their love, intuition, sensitivity, patience and acceptance— whatever has become an integral part of thier lives. Whatever I teach was learned in that spirit. What makes them the most excellent teachers is that they are teaching what they have lived. They are open to experience and experimentation. They are not teaching for superficial purposes to become experts to earn more money and buy luxuries. As a result, there is much less ego involvement, and so much creative energy is released.

As subsequent programs in counseling, bodywork, and massage were offered, Gurudev worked creatively in the design process, teaching the disciples how to incorporate the principles of Kripalu Yoga into every aspect of their work. As he developed and adapted the ideas, he revealed the higher purposes of karma yoga:

To learn to give a massage, or to do any kind of work, you must first reorganize your life to become a proper vehicle for service. Your giving must involve all of your life. You give not only from the level of technique, but also from the level of psyche. Every day you tune into the higher vibration, the unlimited sense of healing energy. In working to become a vehicle for others' transformation, you must first transform yourself. This doesn't mean you must be a saint before you're ready to give a massage, but the process of preparation will impel you towards your own inner attunement to the higher self. With every massage done in this meditative attitude, you become a better person, a little more conscious each time.

In 1979, Gurudev had an insight which was to change the scope of the ashram's service to humanity. For a year the administrative board, composed of senior disciples who headed key departments in the ashram and Fellowship, had been struggling to find a home-based activity that could employ more of the residents. (About half of the residents were then holding jobs in nearby towns.) Almost all felt a deep yearning to be "at home", devoting their creative energies to serving full-time at the ashram.

One morning after his meditation, Gurudev had the inspiration to start a holistic health center. He realized that holistic health would be the most effective way to introduce yoga to people who needed it but were not yet open to its more traditional forms. The services of the center would incorporate the teachings of hatha yoga and raja yoga, adapted to the modern Western approach to healthy living. The center would be set in the framework of the supportive Kripalu environment with a well-qualified, dedicated staff who were practicing Gurudev's teachings.

In that first summer of 1979, the Kripalu Center for Holistic Health opened its doors to more than three hundred guests. Within two years, the number of guests had climbed to more than one thousand. Staff doubled and then tripled as professionally skilled residents (including two medical doctors, a psychologist, and a physical therapist) contributed their energies to the popular and growing center. Homeopathic medicine, massage, polarity, biofeedback, and a full spectrum of healing therapies were offered both in group programs and for individual care.

Guests often share about the effect the Health Center has had on their lives. Bob Barth (Dyanath), an elementary school principal, is one guest who received a new lease on life at the Health Center:

When I first came to Kripalu Center for Holistic Health four years ago, I had just had a heart attack and was on five kinds of medication to keep tranquil, unstressed and relaxed. My cardiologist gave me four weeks to live. At the Health Center, I worked with almost the entire staff, not just on my heart, but on all of the stresses in my life that had led to the attack. The exercises and the breathing techniques that I learned there helped me to achieve deeper feelings of relaxation and control of my circulation. Gradually, I was able to drop all forms of medication. Although my doctor could give no medical explanation for the changes in my body, he was as excited about them as I was.

Has the Kripalu Center for Holistic Health been important in my life? You bet it has. From a four-week lifeline, with a heart attack at the end, to a feeling of total health and relaxation—and getting a whole lot closer to my family—that's a big gift to receive.

Edgar Mitchell, one of three astronauts on the Apollo 14 mission to the moon, was another visitor to the Health Center. Founder of the Institute of Noetic Sciences, he has a long-standing connection with

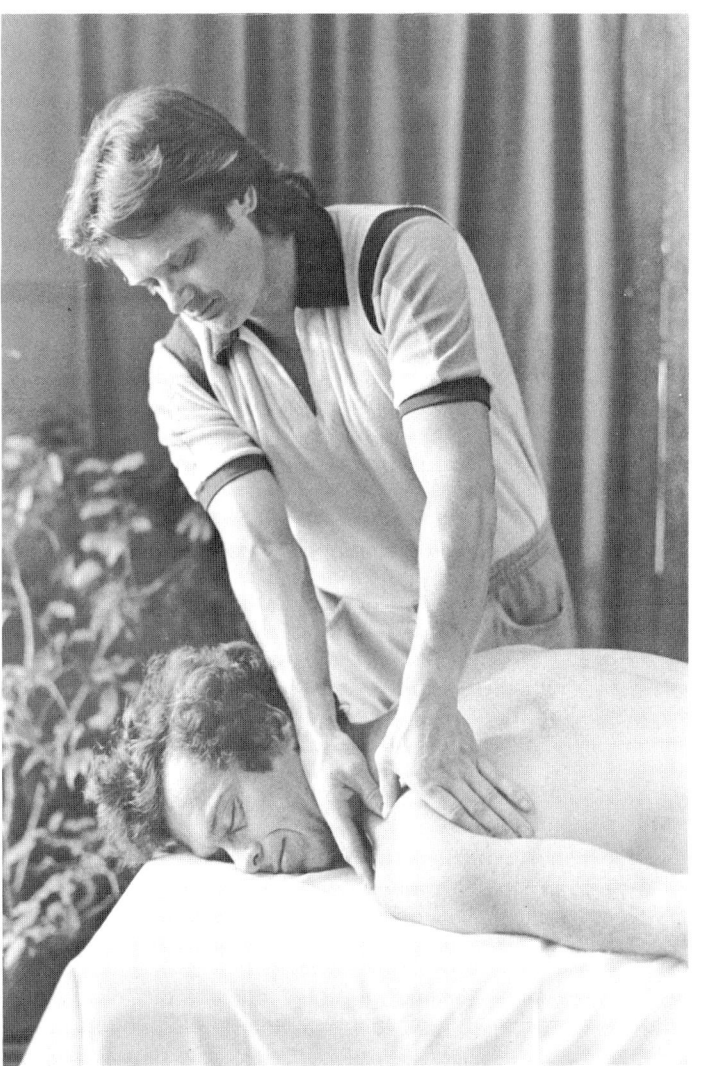

Disciples leading programs and giving health services.

Gurudev:

Almost ten years ago, following my Apollo 14 flight to the moon, I was privileged to meet Yogi Amrit Desai. At that meeting, we discovered our shared interest in a deeper perspective of life, health and spirituality. Yogi Desai was immensely helpful to me through his great understanding of the relationship between health and spiritual discipline. This shared interest has continued over the years, and I have been delighted to visit and benefit from the fruit of his effort at the Kripalu Center for Holistic Health. The warm, caring and thoroughly professional individuals on the staff have been a delight for me to experience. My own sense of well-being and health was greatly enhanced by my stay at the Center.

Yet another appreciative perspective of the Health Center was given by Erich O. Reprich, a writer and newspaper publisher who has lived and worked around the globe—in the Far East, Europe, Canada, and Africa. Fondly known as EO at the Center, he writes eloquently about his experience:

I visited many European spas. They're beautiful places with all the conveniences of a first-class hotel. But I found nothing which compares with the concept of the Health Center—fasting for physical and mental detoxification, Kripalu Yoga, vegetarian diet, personal counseling, and teaching on personal growth. Here everything's combined.

Not in the whole world have I seen so many open and loving people as in this place. It's a different thing to have a relationship with someone who, in the back of his mind, wants something in return. In Toronto, if I invited the Prime Minister to a party, he came. He wanted my support, and I wanted his prestige. But here, it's absolutely different. The Kripalu staff come to me and ask, "What can I do for you?" because they are here to serve. This is something extraordinary.

The scope of the programs continually widened to enfold new approaches to transformation. Gurudev poured his heart into the new programs. Each one became a doorway that provided an opportunity for reaching the potentials of the higher self. Through the different programs, people could enter at the level where they felt comfortable. If someone could attend a "Stop Smoking Clinic" at the Health Center and leave behind not only their cigarettes but also their stress, their fears of loving, and their limiting self-concepts, then the smoking clinic was as much of a spiritual experience as a meditation retreat.

Gurudev's concept of yoga is never limited by the external name or label. There is no limitation to his vision or the disciples' imaginations in creating the vehicles through which help can be extended.

Many new programs have been introduced to open more ways in which people can experience Kripalu Yoga. One such addition was a master's degree program in Holistic Health Studies, sponsored by Goddard College. Those interested in formal graduate education could reside at Kripalu for a fifteen-month program and receive spiritual and professional training for degree certification. Another doorway to growth opened through "Life Seminars"; disciples began traveling all over North America to give weekend workshops in interpersonal relationships, stress management, and holistic health. Following the enthusiastic reception of these seminars, Management Potentials, Inc., a consulting group for large companies, schools, and hospitals, was created. Yogic principles were adapted to the existing needs of corporate and private firms which wanted to train their staffs in health maintenance, communications, and team-building

At right: Disciples leading programs and giving health services.

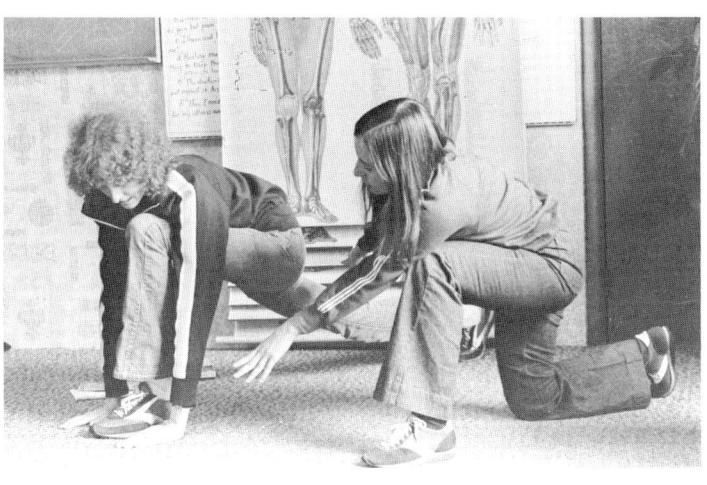
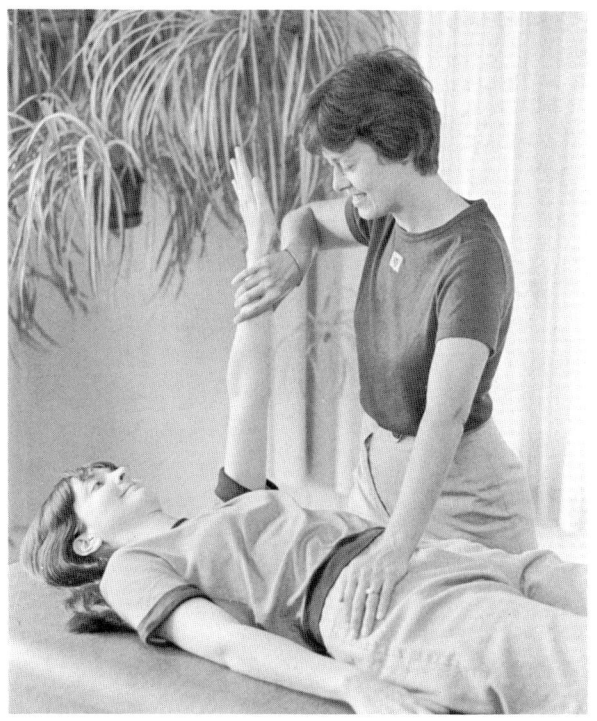

skills.

All of these programs challenged the disciples' creativity and allowed them to extend their capacity for service while integrating Gurudev's teachings more fully into their lives. Every program happened as a living, experiential process rather than as the transfer of theoretical information. Guests were able to move immediately to the level of experiential learning, rather than remaining on a purely intellectual level, and were transformed in the process. Of the thousands who came, many were touched by the magic of love and felt their lives opening to a new potential for happiness, inner freedom, and joy. Over and over they shared with Gurudev and the residents: "If I can only find a way to change my life at home...to carry with me what I've found here."

Those who felt this yearning most deeply often chose to become disciples of Gurudev, although not all became ashram residents. As their numbers increased, nonresident disciples began gathering in their homes with other yoga students and seekers for regular meditation, yoga classes, or satsangs. Joining together for mutual support in their spiritual growth, some of the groups became very large, and the first Kripalu Centers in outlying areas were formed. At first, the groups were self-directed, but with a flood of requests for support and more information, the ashram soon took a guiding hand in becoming a "mother center." A department was formed to serve all who were affiliated with Kripalu by freely offering the basic philosophy, approaches, and guidelines for running the centers. On a recent count, more than thirty-eight Kripalu groups were meeting regularly in the United States, Canada and Europe.

Contact between the Kripalu Retreat and the outlying group is maintained through the **Kripalu Yoga Quest** (the tri-annual newspaper distributed to more than 50,000 people), through Life Seminar workshops, and through Gurudev's frequent lecture tours.

In 1981, Gurudev received a personal invitation from the president of the European Yoga Teachers Federation to speak at their eighth annual meeting. He was a special guest at the week-long conference, along with such noted masters as Swami Shri Satyananda, Swami Shri Chidananda, and Swami Shri Satchidananda. Before an audience of five hundred people, he introduced the principles of Kripalu Yoga and gave experiential seminars to the group. Following a warm reception at the conference, he gave workshops and lectures in Stuttgart, Munich, and Eppstein, Germany.

As Gurudev took the teachings of Kripalu Yoga abroad, the truth of Bapuji's teaching that "The whole world is one family" re-echoed in the hearts and lives of all those who were connected with Kripalu Fellowship. And even as the energy of guru and disciples flowed outward, it was returned many times magnified in the love of those who came "home" to Kripalu.

Among those who honored Gurudev was His Holiness Swami Shri Gangeshwaranandji. In 1982, at the age of 102, he is one of the great spiritual preceptors of the Udasin path, having founded twelve ashrams in India and more than six hundred Ved Mandirs (temples) throughout India and Europe. After experiencing the selfless service and devotion at Kripalu Yoga Retreat with great joy and satisfaction, he conferred the distinguished title of "Maharishi" upon Gurudev with the following message:

I offer this title of Maharishi (Great Sage) in recognition of the many years dedicated in the service of Sanatana Dharma by Yogiraj Amritji. This dedicated acharya has upheld the most ancient truths of the Vedas, through his humanitarian works in North America and India. The total commitment of his life to these ancient principles has truly transformed the wisdom of these great scriptures into a language of love, enabling thousands of Western aspirants to deeply recognize and integrate the highest spiritual teachings into their lives.

May the Lord eternally guide, protect, and bless his spiritual works, gracing him with deepening wisdom, expanding clarity and ever-growing devotion to God.

9·Truth Shines Like the Sun

Living in the flow of time, Gurudev has become a flute through which the music of universal love and transformation plays to the hearts of mankind. From the shy and loving boy in Gujarat to a teacher whose message is recognized by thousands and honored by saints, his life is an inspiration for all those who journey on the inner path. The external achievements of his life have not dimmed the initial fire of his spiritual yearning nor the primal awareness with which he experiences each moment. For Gurudev, it has all come from God. Like a gracious host, he entertains what God sends him with deep gratitude and acceptance. With equal ease he welcomes the new and relinquishes the old.

In many ways he has maintained, effortlessly and without struggle, the simple and unpretentious way of life he learned as a boy: love and acceptance of others, compassion and care for the needy, and the wholehearted embrace of life in its moment-to-moment fullness. Adjusting, adapting and reverberating harmoniously with life, day by day, the young Indian boy with limitless vision has opened himself to a universe of service rich in possibilities, endless in potential. What has emerged, through the grace of God and Bapuji, is the enlightened master, the beloved guru, the dispeller of darkness and bringer of light.

Yet, unbound by the role of guru, he exists in a world of inner freedom, completely absorbed with the situation, the person, or the event unfolding in each moment before him. He is never burdened by the demands on his life, whether he is planning the relocation of the Retreat and Ashram to another, larger facility or fulfilling the legacy of Bapuji's work in India.* He sees these demands on him simply as additional opportunites for growth and service, a naturally expanding field in which to channel the teachings of Kripalu Yoga.

Gurudev shares the perspective that has allowed him inner freedom to grow in response to the unexpected turns of his life.

Rather than plan a goal for myself to achieve something specific, I plan only my direction. When we limit ourselves with goals, we are placing a dead-end on our growth and

---

*Bapuji left Gurudev the legacy of carrying on his spiritual work at Kayavarohan and other ashrams in India. This request for Gurudev's commitment in India was written shortly before Bapuji's Mahasamadhi.

inhibiting the flow. A goal is the end of external achievement, but when our eyes are fixed on inner transformation, the goal is only to be in the present. Each project or happening will have an end, but the ending is only one point in the infinite process of life.

In Kripalu Yoga, inner growth is the focus; the goal is incidental. The process is to explore the infinite potentials of life, and the work is only a vehicle for that exploration. Such work, where we are constantly aware of the process and do not become addicted to end results, is a true sadhana.

Gurudev's life, with its inspired union of intention and action, is itself the truth through which his disciples discover themselves. His higher consciousness, through which he sees all problems as the beginning of solutions and all pain as the beginning of deeper understanding, allows his energy to flow freely and lovingly into teaching his spiritual children. He is perpetually finding new aspects of himself to deal with the ever-changing conditions of his service. His lack of attachment to a role, a way of being, or to his achievements, gives him a depth and spontaneity that defies definition. The events of his life, and the record of the impact that he has had on others, give a strong impression of who he is. However, Gurudev's essence—the spirit of love that reaches out and touches everyone in his presence—can only be experienced directly. To grasp the truth of who Gurudev is, one must join him in the openness to life that he embodies.

My life is a perpetually unfolding, evolving process, constantly moving from the known to the unknown. There is nothing good, nothing bad. I am there with whatever is given me. Moving with life, I am a perpetually flowing, changing entity. There are no limits because I do not get stuck in any beliefs or thoughts of who I am, who others are, or what I know and don't know. I simply stay in the flow of life where the truth is revealed to me from moment to moment. That truth shines like a sun.

JAI GURUDEV

Yogi Amrit Desai: A Chronology

1932	Born in Halol, Gujarat Province, India, Oct. 16.
1932-42	Early years in Pratappura, 10 miles from Halol. Primary school in nearby village of Shankarpura.
1941	Critically ill with typhoid for 3 months.
1942	Moves to Halol, with his family.
1944-51	Attends the M.S. High School, Halol.
1947	Meets Swami Shri Kripalvanandji (Bapuji) in Halol.
1951-52	Studies engineering at Kalabhavan Technical Institute, Baroda.
1952	Art teacher, Jarod High School, Halol.
1953-54	Trains with the Indian Air Force, Madras.
1954-55	Teaches at Mobharoad Vakal High School.
1955	Marries Urmila (Mataji) Jan. 29.
1955-56	Studies at Seth C.N. School of Art, Ahmedabad. Studies Hindi literature at Gujarati College, Ahmedabad.
1956	Receives Drawing Teacher's Certificate (Government of Bombay).
1956-60	Teaches at St. Xavier's High School, Ahmedabad.
1958	Death of father, Chimanlal Desai (Jan. 7, 1876-Apr. 26, 1958).
1959	Birth of first son, Pragnesh, Sept. 5.
1960	Arrives in the United States, Feb. 5. Lives at the International House, Philadelphia. Begins teaching yoga classes, the first held in Philadelphia. Student at Philadelphia College of Art (1960-1964) Employment at Fred Whitaker Co., American Bag and Paper Corp.
1961	Represents India in a yoga presentation before 2000 at International House Day, Bellevue-Stratford Hotel, Mar. 10. Arrival of Mataji, Pragnesh and Shanti from India, Aug. 13. Art exhibition at John Wanamaker. Numerous radio and television appearances.
1962	Represents India at International House Day, presenting legend of Krishna and Radha through art, narration and flute music, Feb. 23. Birth of second son, Malay, Nov. 19.
1963-66	Textile designer at Masland Duraleather.
1964	B.F.A. in commercial art, Philadelphia College of Art.
1966	First trip back to India since arriving in America. Travel through Europe by car, visiting 13 countries, with Mataji, Pragnesh, Malay, and Shanti.

	Founds Yoga Society of Pennsylvania, in Philadelphia.
1968	Birth of daughter, Yogini, March 13.
1969	Five-month trip to India for intensive study with Bapuji, May 3-Sept. 7. American students accompany him on part of the trip.
	Receives title of Yogi from His Holiness Swami Shri Kripalvanandji (Bapuji) in a special celebration.
1970	Experiences first spontaneous yoga posture flow.
	Invited to speak at Atlanta Pop Festival.
	Participates in controlled laboratory experiments at Jefferson Memorial Hospital: Underwent tests to demonstrate that a human can control and modify organic functions of the involuntary nervous system.
	Founds Kripalu Yoga Ashram, Sumneytown, Pa.
	Invited to speak at World Conference on Scientific Yoga, New Delhi, Dec. 19-23.
1971	Attends festival in India during which Bapuji gives first speech in 12 years to 25,000 people, Jan. 4.
	Receives Shaktipat Diksha from Bapuji, Jan. 7.
	Gives lecture at Spiritual Frontiers Association, Chicago.
	Honorary Doctor of Philosophy conferred by the Florida Research Institute.
	Yoga Society conducts 150 classes per week, training over 2500 students in each 10-week course.
	Guest speaker at Earth Day in Fairmont Park, Philadelphia.
1972	Leads numerous seminars, meditations, workshops, yoga classes.
	Directs and assists renovations made at the Sumneytown Ashram.
	Moves into the Sumneytown ashram with his family and several disciples.
1973	Gives presentation at Yoga Convention held at Watson Homestead, N.Y.
	Begins three month period of silence, seclusion and intensive sadhana at Sumneytown ashram, Dec. 9.
1974	Accompanied by 60 disciples, attends dedication ceremonies of Brahmeshwar Temple, Kayavarohan.
	Honorary Doctor of Yoga Science awarded by His Holiness Jagadguru Shankaracharya Maharaj, at Dakor, India, May 11.
	Forms Kripalu Yoga Fellowship, a non-profit religious organization.
	Appears on "Mike Douglas Show" (NBC).
	Death of mother, Bhuriben Desai, (Apr. 19, 1911-Oct. 24, 1974).
1975	Gives ten-day ashram-sponsored Sadhana Retreat at Ursinus College, Pa.

Appears in "Search for Something Else" (ABC).

Receives title of Acharya Pravaraha (Supreme Spiritual Teacher), awarded by Swami Shri Vedavyasanandji, October.

Purchases Kripalu Yoga Retreat, Summit Station, Pa., December.

1976 Dedication of Kripalu Yoga Retreat, officiated by Swami Shri Satchidananda and other noted guests, May 29.

1977 Visited Bapuji in India.

Establishes charitable trust for educating students in India.

Bapuji arrives in America, May.

1978 Master's Degree Program established at Kripalu.

1979 Visits India to assist in publication of Bapuji's books.

Opens the Holistic Health Center at Kripalu Yoga Retreat, providing group programs and individual services in holistic health.

Founds Management Potentials, Inc. to provide training and consultation services to businesses in the areas of stress management and corporate wellness.

Receives title of "Yogiraj" by Shri Chandra Swami Maharaj.

1980 Gives first European seminars in France and Germany.

Receives title of Yogacharya from His Holiness Swami Shri Kripalvanandji (Bapuji) at Kripalu Yoga Ashram, July 26.

Makes pilgrimage to India inspired by Bapuji, to visit ashrams and spiritual teachers.

1981 Keynote speaker, European Federation of Yoga Teachers Conference, Zinal, Switzerland.

Returns to India with Bapuji, Sept.

Bapuji's Mahasamadhi, Dec. 29.

1982 Attends Bapuji's Mahasamadhi ceremony in India, Jan. 13.

Awarded title of Maharishi by His Holiness Swami Shri Gangeshwaranandji, July 28.

50th birthday celebration, Oct. 16.

Titles and Degrees

1964 Bachelor of Fine Arts Degree, Philadelphia College of Art.

1969 Title of Yogi, conferred by His Holiness Swami Shri Kripalvanandji (Bapuji), in recognition of significant knowledge and practice of the principles of yoga.

1971 Honorary Doctor of Philosophy, Florida Research Institute

1974 Doctor of Yoga Science, awarded by His Holiness Jagadguru Shankaracharya Maharaj, spiritual leader of Hinduism. The degree signifies outstanding contributions to humanity and the knowledge of yoga. It is an honor that has been given only to a few choice individuals during the long ministry of the Shankaracharya.

1975 Acharya Pravaraha (Supreme Spiritual Teacher) awarded by Swami Vedavyasanandji, prelate of over 300,000 Hindu monks and Chancellor of Rishikul Sanskrit University in Hardwar, India. The ancient ceremony was held for the first time on American soil at the Sumneytown Ashram. This title gives Gurudev the authority to preside over marriages, funerals, and religious ceremonies.

1979 Shri Yogiraj Amritji, awarded by Shri Chandra Swami Maharaj, the great Indian seer, spiritual leader and Founding Director of the Sarva Dharma Sambhava Center, (an international spiritual organization dedicated to furthering the cause of world peace by fostering greater understanding between all religious traditions). The title was given in recognition of Yogi Desai's work to build a deeper understanding in America of India's cultural heritage.

1980 Title of Yogacharya (Spiritual Preceptor) conferred by His Holiness Swami Shri Kripalvanandji (Bapuji) in honor of Yogi Desai's years of intensive study, teaching and practice of the philosophy and spiritual principles of yoga.

1982 Title of Maharishi (Great Sage) awarded by His Holiness Ved-Darshanacharya Sadguru Swami Gangeshwaranandji Maharaj Udasin, spiritual preceptor of the Udasin path, founder of twelve ashrams in India and 600 Ved Mandirs (temples).

Art Awards and Exhibits

1962 First Prize, Indoor Arts Festival, Newtown Square, Pa.

Third Prize, Meadowbrook School Fair Art Exhibit, Meadowbrook, Pa.

First Prize, Ellisburg Circle Art Show, Erlton, Pa.

1963 First Prize, Vineland Art Show, Vineland, N.J.

First Prize, Feasterville Art Exhibit, Feasterville, Pa.

Gold Medal, Best Male Artist, Newtown Square Art Exhibit, Newtown Square, Pa.

One Man Show: Watercolors, Handwoven & Hand Printed Fabrics, World Affairs Council, Philadelphia, Pa.

Two Man Show, Philadelphia Art Alliance Competitive Exhibition

Guest Artist: Handwoven & Silk-Screen Printed Fabrics and Watercolors, Arts Guild, Episcopal Academy, Philadelphia, Pa.

Two Man Show, Park Art Gallery, Philadelphia, Pa.

1964 One Man Show, Little Gallery, Philadelphia, Pa.

One Man Show, Watercolors, Philadelphia International House

First Prize, Vineland Art Show, Vineland, N.J. (pictured at right)

First Prize, Atlantic City Boardwalk Show, Atlantic City, N.J.

1965 One Man Show, Wallingford Art Center, Wallingford, Pa.

Best of Show, Prentiss Huckins Medal, Lansdale, Pa.

Art League Show, Lansdale, Pa.

Philadelphia Museum of Art, Regional Drawing Exhibit

American Watercolor Society, 98th Annual, New York, N.Y.

Philadelphia Academy of Music, Tribute to Philadelphia Chamber Orchestra Society

Second Prize, Greater New York Outdoor Art Exhibit, New York, N.Y.

Second Prize, Atlantic City Boardwalk Show, Atlantic City, N.J.

Certificate of Merit - ADVAC Regional Art Exhibit, Commercial Museum, Philadelphia, Pa.

1966 One Man Show, Echeverria Art Gallery, Morristown, N.J.

One Man Show, LaSalle College, Philadelphia, Pa.

One Man Show, Pennsylvania Military College, Chester, Pa.

Two Man Show, Ligoa Duncan Gallery, New York, N.Y.

1967 One Man Show, Friends Central School, Philadelphia, Pa.

1968 One Man Show, Springfield Library, Springfield, Pa.

Glossary of Sanskrit Terms

arti—a light ceremony which symbolically honors the Divine Light within.

asanas—hatha yoga postures.

ashram—a spiritual retreat, usually the home of a spiritual master.

Bapuji—"Dear Father," the name affectionately given to Swami Shri Kripalvanandji.

bhajan—a devotional song or hymn.

brahmacharya—literally, actions which lead to Brahma or God. Usually refers to the practice of celibacy and moderation of all the senses.

Brahman—the Absolute, supreme power and ultimate reality of the universe.

chakras—the seven psychic, spiritual centers of man's energy.

Dadaji—"dear Grandfather," the familiar name given to the guru of Bapuji.

darshan—a meeting or audience with a spiritual master.

guru—literally, dispeller of darkness; a spiritual master.

Guru Purnima—an annual celebration performed in honor of the guru.

Gurudev—a respectful way of addressing one's guru.

japa—repetition of a mantra as a meditation technique, using a rosary of 108 beads, called a mala.

karma—the universal law of action and reaction; cause and effect.

karma yoga—the yoga of action; usually referring to work performed selflessly for spiritual growth.

Kripalu—the compassionate one; the merciful one.

kriya—a yogic movement or technique performed for physical, emotional or mental purification; often occurs spontaneously during deeper spiritual practices.

kundalini—a powerful evolutionary energy lying dormant at the base of the spine, usually awakened only through intense spiritual practice with a guru.

kundalini yoga—a scientific branch of yoga designed to activate the energy of kundalini and channel it creatively for higher spiritual consciousness.

Lakulish—Bapuji's guru; represented by a stone lingam at Kayavarohan.

lingam—a cylindrical stone column, rounded at the top, symbolizing Lord Shiva.

mantra—sacred words or sounds that can be repeated as a meditation technique to still the mind.

prana—the vital life force or life energy in man.

puja—a ceremony of love and reverence for the spiritual master, involving offerings of incense, flowers, water and light.

sadhak—a spiritual aspirant; a practitioner of yoga.

sadhana—spiritual practices.

samadhi—a high state of spiritual consciousness in which the aspirant experiences oneness with God.

sanatan dharma—the ancient Indian path or religion of eternal truth, promoting love for the family and service to humanity.

satsang—a spiritual gathering, often in the presence of the guru.

seva—selfless service carried out in service of the higher self.

shakti—the creative, transformative energy or power within man.

shaktipat diksha—the transmission of spiritual energy from guru to disciple.

shastras—ancient Indian scriptures outlining ways to the realization of truth.

siddhas—psychic powers developed through yogic practices.

tapas—spiritual practices which purify the mind, emotions and body; literally, the spiritual fire which burns the aspirant's impurities.

Vedas—one of the ancient scriptures of India.

yoga—union; self-integration and self-realization so the individual consciousness merges with the universal energy (God).

Further Reading

BOOKS BY YOGI AMRIT DESAI

Guru and Disciple: A Relationship of Love, 1975.

Shaktipat Kundalini Yoga: Frequently Asked Questions, 1975.

God Is Energy: Five Articles on Kundalini Yoga, 1976.

Love Is Like the Sun: Meditative Reflections, 1976.

Love: A Flight From Addiction to Freedom, 1976.

Kripalu Yoga: Meditation in Motion, 1981.

Happiness Is Now: Reflective Writings of Yogi Amrit Desai, edited by Gray Ward, 1982.

(All books published by the Kripalu Yoga Fellowship, Summit Station, Pa.)

ARTICLES BY YOGI AMRIT DESAI

"Journey to the Sacred Self," *Yes, It's Love: Your Life Can Be a Miracle*, edited by Orest Bedrij, 1974, pp. 23-28.

"Path to the Divine" and "God is Energy," *Inner Paths*, Nov. 1977, pp. 30-32 and 34-35 respectively.

"Guru and Disciple," *Many Paths*, Nov. 1977, pp. 1-6.

"The Disciples' Love," *Eclipse*, May-June 1979, pp. 14-15.

"Kundalini Yoga Through Shaktipat," *Kundalini, Evolution and Enlightenment*, edited by John White, Anchor Press, 1979, pp. 69-75.

Plus articles in *Yoga Jyoti*, (1967-75) published by Yoga Society of Pennsylvania, and in *Kripalu Yoga Quest* and *Guru Prasad*, published by the Kripalu Yoga Fellowship.

ARTICLES AND BOOKS ON YOGI AMRIT DESAI

Butler, D.R., "Instant Cosmic Consciousness?", *Kundalini, Evolution and Enlightenment*, edited by John White, Anchor Press, 1979, pp. 184-188.

Finnegan, Gita, "Kripalu Ashram, an Experiment in Love," *Communities*, March-April, 1975, pp. 7-9.

Lee, Virginia, "Kripalu Yoga: Meditation in Motion," *Yoga Journal*, July-August, 1980, pp. 40-48.

Rajendra, *Journey to the New Age*, Kripalu Yoga Fellowship, 1976.

Vlanis, Gregory, "Interview With Yogi Amrit Desai," *Movement Newspaper*, September 1982.

RELATED BOOKS

Kripalvanandji, Swami Shri, *Science of Meditation*, New Karnodaya Press, Bombay, 1977.

_____, *Premyatra, Books I & II*, Kripalu Yoga Fellowship, 1981-82.

Muni, Rajarshi, *Light From Guru to Disciple*, Kripalu Yoga Ashram, 1974.

Staff of Kripalu Center for Holistic Health, *The Self-Health Guide: A Personal Program for Holistic Living*, Kripalu Yoga Fellowship, 1980.

Staff of Kripalu Yoga Retreat, *Bapuji in America: Darshans at Kripalu Ashram*, Kripalu Yoga Fellowship, 1979.

For more information on
Kripalu Center for Yoga and Health,
write or call:
P. O. Box 793
Lenox, MA 01240
(413) 448-3400